GROWING UP NORTH

True Adventures of Free-Range Children

Written by

Elaine Brunet Fredrikson

©2019 Elaine Brunet Fredrikson

All rights reserved

ISBN: 9781704830476

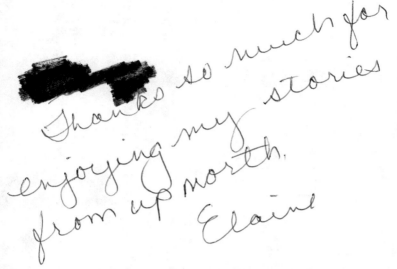

Thanks so much for enjoying my stories from up north,
Elaine

This book is dedicated in memory of our dear brother David, without whom I would never have thought to become a writer.

Thanks for your wonderful imagination and creativity.

We miss you, David.

Introduction

As a substitute teacher I often fill gaps in assignments with stories from my past and found that the students love hearing them. I became the "story-telling teacher."

Students run up to me at the beginning of the day and ask excitedly, "Are you our sub today?" They're always disappointed if I have to tell them that I'm there for another teacher.

The students sit mesmerized as I regale them with stories of my childhood.

They all agreed, "You've gotta' write these stories down and we want a copy of the book when you're done! Can you tell us the treehouse story again?"

This book was originally intended for young students, but I have found that the adults probably love them even more because they lived in the same era.

I've received comments such as; "I laughed out loud at _____ (they all loved a different story).

"This took me right back to my childhood."

"I grew up on a farm, so I really appreciated the farm stories."

I hope you enjoy these stories no matter what your age.

Growing Up North

Prologue

    Life doesn't always turn out the way you want it to. Sometimes it's better; sometimes it's worse. What's important is to accept life the way it is and find a way to make the best of each moment.
    My life began on the worst end since my mother died before my 2nd birthday. Because of her death, we moved frequently in the first five years of my life. At the time, it was decided by the Child Welfare Department that men were not supposed to raise little girls on their own, so my early life was spent dodging the CWD by moving from one relative's home to another. I stayed with my grandparents up in Chisholm on occasion, but mostly I lived between two sets of aunts and uncles as well as my paternal grandmother. The aunts and uncles were wonderful people, and since none of them had any children of their own, they provided me with lots of healthy attention. Both sets of aunts and uncles were more than willing to adopt me as their own, but Dad wasn't

so sure he was willing to split up the family. Dad decided he needed to do something permanent in order to keep the family together.

But let me back up a bit so you understand how all of this happened.

Chapter 1

In the Beginning

We lived on the border of western South Dakota and eastern Wyoming in the small town of Belle Fourche (pronounced Bell Foosh).

Back in the late 1800's it was once a large cattle shipping town for the west due to the rail yard that went through town. (You may have heard it mentioned in several of the great old western movies.) Belle Fourche soon became the largest livestock shipping point in the world, shipping cattle from coast to coast.

During the time we lived there, the cattle were no longer driven into town by cowboys on horseback but rather by train or semi-truck. It still serves as an important livestock auction center in the west as well as a wool shipping center. It also serves as the center of a bentonite mining industry and that's how we ended up there.

Dad was an electrician in the iron ore mines of northern Minnesota, and the bentonite mines in Wyoming offered Dad an opportunity for employment and a new adventure away from my Aunt Martha (Mom's sister).

My mother was diagnosed with a brain tumor while she was expecting me, so immediately after I was born, my parents were rushed to the Mayo Clinic in Rochester, Minnesota, to allow the doctors to begin treating her illness. My brothers and I stayed behind with friends from church until Mom's health improved and we could get back to Minnesota to resume a normal life once again.

It was early in March when my Aunt Martha and Uncle Royal drove out to South Dakota to pick us up and bring us back to their home in Hibbing, Minnesota. As is typical of early spring weather in South Dakota, Royal and Martha had to drive across the entire state through a raging blizzard. It was a wild prairie blizzard where the road often disappeared under the snow for several minutes at a time. It blew so hard the wind whistled through the car windows and sounded like the screams of some deranged animal. Often the front of the car disappeared in the snow and all that could be seen was white nothing! My uncle held his breath until the road reappeared and he knew he was still on the right path. Royal was a bit of a wild man who loved a challenge and the chance to drive no matter what the conditions were, so he was thrilled to be a part of this crazy adventure. Besides, he was on a mission to pick up "his" kids. The roads across northern South Dakota are nothing more than two lane highways and the ranches are few and far between.

My uncle knew there was only one chance to get this right or they would end up freezing to death in a ditch.

"Royal, slow down! You can't even see the road through this blizzard!" pleaded Martha.

With a determined look in his eyes, my uncle said, "Don't worry, this is just one long straight road. There are no turns, so I just have to go perfectly straight all the way to western South Dakota. I just have to make sure I don't turn the wheel – at all," my uncle said confidently.

As the wind whipped and the snow blew across the road, my uncle gripped the steering wheel until his knuckles turned white with tension. He leaned into the windshield and strained his eyes through his thick glasses in an effort to see the highway ahead.

My aunt cried and prayed and prayed and cried. "Royal, please stop! I can't take this anymore! We have to get to Belle Fourche alive so we can bring the kids home!"

"The kids will be fine, and we'll make it there in one piece. Don't you worry. Besides, there's no place to stop for another 100 miles. We have to keep going!"

At last they arrived in Belle Fourche and my aunt practically collapsed through the door of my parent's friends, Tom and Karen, who were taking care of me while Mom and Dad were gone. The boys were spending their time with a family named Lemm.

"I can't believe you drove all the way across the entire state of South Dakota in this blizzard!" exclaimed Tom, "You must be nuts!"

"Just a little snow – nothing we haven't seen in Minnesota before," said Royal.

"Where is the baby?"

"Here she is," Karen cooed as she entered the room carrying me.

"What a chunk! Just look at those cheeks!" Martha exclaimed.

"She's absolutely beautiful!" Royal said almost breathlessly as he gazed on my chubby little face. I giggled and in his mind I would always be his little girl.

We spent the night with the couple and enjoyed the warmth, good food and hospitality of Tom and Karen. Royal regaled them with the story of driving through the blizzard.

Finally, it was time for bed, and we all went upstairs for a good night's sleep.

The next morning the snow was still coming down hard and blowing like crazy. "We'd better get packed up if we're going to make it across the state by dark," Royal announced.

"What?" said Tom. "You're not planning to go out in this weather again, are you? We've had at least another foot of snow since you arrived, and the wind is still blowing over forty miles an hour. You can't possibly drive home in this! Just stay here with us until this storm breaks."

"Thanks, Tom," Royal said, "but you and Karen have done enough. We really appreciate you looking after a newborn for so long – I know that isn't easy given the nightly feedings and crying and all."

"She was no trouble at all – such a good baby. I sure hope Elna is going to be alright. We're all praying for her and Paul and the kids."

"We've missed having a baby in the house. Are you sure you won't stay until the storm passes? We have plenty of room and I'd sure hate to hear that anything happened to you on your way home. Please stay another night. For the sake of the whole family. Lord knows Paul and Elna don't need to be worrying about your safety and their three kids."

"We'll be fine," Royal said. "I'm used to driving in snow – we get plenty of it up north. We'd better be going so we don't lose any daylight. Thanks again. We sure appreciate all you've done, and we'll call when we make it home. I think we'll find a place on the other end of the state to stay for tonight and continue home in the morning so we can get there before dark. Would you mind calling the Lemms to let them know we're on our way to pick up the boys?"

"I have enough bottles of formula made up for Elaine as well as a bag of clean clothes and diapers. I also have a sack for the soiled diapers that you can put in the trunk so you don't have to smell them all the way home," Karen said.

My uncle shook Tom's hand and Martha hugged Karen and we were off on my second adventure (you have to consider being born a first adventure even if you don't know it at the time).

We drove to Spearfish to pick up the boys. Martha and Royal thanked the Lemms ever so much for caring for them and we were on our way.

The snow was getting pretty deep by the time we got in the car with our belongings and headed down the road. There were no such things as infant car seats or seat belts yet, so my aunt and uncle set me in a large cardboard box with plenty of blankets to keep me warm and safe. The wind was blowing hard, but it mercifully kept the snow from piling too high on the roads. Royal had put chains on the tires so we wouldn't slide (there were no radials or snow tires at this time either). Although they were hard on tires, the chains actually allowed for pretty good traction and managed to keep the car on the road. About two hours down the road, Martha began praying and crying again. Still twelve hours of driving ahead. I lay in my box in the back seat between my brothers, cooing and giggling every time the car would swerve.

The sun was beginning to set and we were nearly to the Minnesota border so we stopped at a small town to find a place to stay for the night. The town's restaurant was still open, so they were able to warm a bottle for me and get supper for everyone else. I guzzled it down with gusto and fell fast asleep until I was hungry again in the middle of the night.

Of course, I needed to eat while we were on the road too. Royal was always inventing new ways of doing things, so he came up with a creative way to warm my bottles. When there were no restaurants available, he wrapped the bottles carefully in one of my clean cloth diapers and tied them to the manifold of the engine. Once they were firmly secured, he drove until the bottle was warm, pulled the car over to retrieve it so Martha could feed me, and then continued down the road. Worked like a charm!

After more than two days on the road we finally made it to Hibbing safe and sound. After calling Tom and Karen and the Lemms to let them know we were okay, Martha settled me into what was to be my room for the time being and the boys were bedded downstairs. Several months later, Mom and Dad came home from the Mayo Clinic and my brothers and I went to live with them in the neighboring town of Chisholm.

Chapter 2

Saying Goodbye

Mom didn't make it.

There wasn't much that could be done for cancer back in the early 50's, and in spite of the best efforts of the doctors, the cancer was stronger than she was.

When the boys came home from school one day, Dad met them in the entryway. "Boys, sit down, I need to talk to you. Dad pursed his lips and his mouth twisted in an attempt not to cry. His eyes welled with tears. Your mother died during the night." The boys stood looking at Dad without a word. Finally, David boldly asked, "Where is she?"

"They took her to the mortuary to get her ready for the funeral."

Now, you have to know that parents of the 50's (and earlier) didn't always do things with their children's best interest in mind. They were of the "children should be seen and not heard" generation, so children were rarely allowed to speak their minds in matters of the heart – or any other time. This was one of those moments where parents today would have taken a serious interest in their child's emotional state to help them get through the loss of their mother. Maybe put them in a grief group for kids. Or in therapy so they could get over this traumatic occasion. Not Dad.

"The funeral is Thursday, so I've arranged for you boys and Elaine to go down to Beratto's to play. I don't want you at the funeral because you might cry and upset everyone."

I don't think my brothers ever got over the fact that they were not allowed to cry or go to the funeral home to say good-bye to our mother.

"Don't cry – you need to be strong for your dad," Martha would say. Now keep in mind that the boys were five and seven years old when this happened. How were they not supposed to cry?

Chapter 3

A New Normal

Dad hired housekeepers to help with the day-to-day chores of cooking, cleaning and taking care of the three of us. This had always been "woman's work" so men were pretty incompetent when it came to such things.

We stayed in the same house for another year or so before moving across town.

For as long as I can remember, there was a bully that lived next door who loved to jump me at every opportunity. He waited for me in the bushes next to our front door. The moment I stepped down to the sidewalk he would pounce like a cat and punch me until finally he would run off when my screaming got too loud or my brothers came running out the door to chase him away.

"Dad, that stupid Mikey beats Elaine up every day," Danny said. "Can't we beat *him* up and teach him a lesson?"

"No, boys, that's not the way to solve anything. Just keep an eye on your sister and don't let him hit her anymore," Dad said.

Dad went next door to talk to Mikey's father.

"Now why would my son do such a thing?" His father defended. "She's three years old, do you really think he would beat up a little girl?"

"Well, according to all three children, yes he would, and apparently he does, every time Elaine goes out the front door.

"That's absolutely ridiculous, he would never do such a thing."

The little brat stood behind his father smirking and sticking his tongue out at us while his father continued to tell us what a good boy his son was.

We all knew better.

Finally, one day David and Danny decided they had had enough. Time to teach Mikey a lesson even if Dad didn't think it was right. They decided to set a trap for sweet little Michael – one that would make him think twice before attacking their little sister again. They took stock of all the weapons they had in their toy box.

"How about a sling shot? Or we could try out the bows and arrows we made last week? Maybe a rock to the head would knock some sense into him," said Danny.

"No, we don't really want to hurt him – just let him know he isn't welcome near our house," David said.

Danny thought for a while and said, "If only we had some water balloons."

"We don't have any money for water balloons," David sighed. After a few minutes of thinking, he said,

"I know! Let's go around the neighborhood and collect pop bottles and take them to the grocery store for the deposit money!" David was a genius!

The boys put me in their red wagon and told the housekeeper where we were going, and we were off in search of empty pop bottles.

Money was always tight, so pop bottles were a kid's saving grace when they needed to buy something. They could be returned to the store for 2 cents apiece! "Let's go to the store and find out how much money we need," David suggested. "Hmmm, 12 cents. I think we can do that".

We spent the better part of the day going door-to-door and checking the alleys for bottles. When we finally collected enough, we went to the corner grocery and cashed them in.

The boys filled all fifty of the balloons with water, sent me in the house, and we waited for Mikey to come over for his daily game of "I think it's time to go beat up the little kid next door." Little did he know that today he would get a taste of his own medicine!

As soon as the boys saw Mikey sneak over to our house and settle in the bushes waiting for me, they crouched in wait on the other side of the steps, trying hard to keep from giggling.

Sure enough, just as I came out the door, Mikey jumped out of the bushes and ran to me.

Just then, Danny and David jumped up from the other side of the steps and yelled, "Your turn, Mikey!"

They pelted little Mikey with the balloons with all their might! Mikey was soaked and stinging from the balloons! Hah!

I have to say I basked in the glory of watching him get pelted and running home in tears!

According to Dad, the boys were not supposed to touch Mikey in order to solve the beating problem, so they found another way for revenge! Dad didn't say they couldn't use water balloons on him. Right?

Mikey screamed and cried like a little baby and went running home leaving a trail of water and dead balloons behind him.

The boys jumped and shouted with joy and I joined in the celebration although I wasn't really sure what had just happened. Several of the balloons broke as the boys were about to lob them at Mikey so in the end, everyone was soaking wet.

"Yeah, run home, you big baby!" Danny called after him.

"And don't touch our sister ever again!" David said boldly.

Suddenly the door to Mikey's house flew open and his mother burst through the front door and ran to the boys. She grabbed each of them by their t-shirts and screamed, "What have you little brats done to my boy?" Her face was so close to theirs that the boys could smell cigarettes and a hint of alcohol on her foul breath. She shook them both and yelled, "Answer me! Why would you do that?"

David finally took a deep breath, and even though it meant talking back to an adult, said, "We have had enough of Mikey beating up our little sister every time she goes outside. It was time he learned a lesson!"

Mikey's mother raised her hand at David to slap him across the face when Hazel, our housekeeper, came running out to see what was going on. Hazel loved us like a grandmother, and she had clearly had enough of dear little Michael and both of his parents.

"Enough!" She shouted. We all jumped. "You need to watch your son better and keep him out of our yard! He is a mean little brat and needs a good spanking if you ask me. If he shows up in our yard again, I am just the person who will give it to him!" With that she got right into Mikey's face and said, "Now go home! And don't let me catch you over here again, young man, or you'll have to deal with *me*!"

Good old Hazel! She was as sweet as candy, but don't let anyone bother "her kids" or her wrath would be all over them!

Mikey's mother stood there, open mouthed – not sure of what to say. "Come on, son, we're going home," she said as they turned and stomped away. We watched them walk across the lawn and go in the front door of their house.

David and Danny were feeling fine over their defeat but dreading having to face Dad when he got home from work. They knew he would find out what happened. Sure enough, Hazel told us all to sit down while she explained the whole situation to Dad.

Dad looked sternly at the boys and said, "Boys, I told you I didn't want you to be mean to Mikey in order to solve the problem. Violence doesn't solve anything."

"You said we couldn't beat him up," Danny said. "We didn't touch him – just gave him a good soaking."

And then my dad did something we didn't expect; a smile crept across his face and he laughed out loud! Maybe it was the look of fear on the faces of three little kids or the fact that he thought our plan was brilliant. At any rate, we knew we were in the clear and that made us smile too – mostly out of relief!

"I've got to hand it to you boys, you sure found a perfect answer to the problem. I appreciate you sticking up for your little sister, but from now on I think you just need to stay away from Mikey. You should know that I am very proud of both of you." With that he gave us all a hug and sent us out to play in the back yard.

From that day on, Mikey ran into his house whenever we were outside.

Chapter 4

A New Home

For some reason, we moved across town the fall of the Mikey problem. Maybe it was too difficult for my dad to be in the same home where our mother had lived with us. Too many memories.

I missed living close to the elementary school. It was surrounded by wonderfully fragrant pine trees and we could hide under the huge, low hanging boughs and make forts.

Our new house was yellow and had a great enclosed porch, so we learned to make *new* forts. There were always blankets and sofa cushions that made great "rooms" and mazes. The new house was a hit!

The best part though was that there was a boy (Gary) and girl (Nita) who lived across the street to play with. Unlike Mikey, they were really nice!

Although Nita was a true tomboy, I could sometimes get her to play dolls with me. At any rate, we had lots of fun together. I had never had a girl friend before!

Gary, Danny and David spent their days fishing, pretend hunting and exploring whenever they could. It didn't take long for them to become great friends.

Gary and Nita's mom was really nice too. She would let all three of us spend the night at their house on occasion and she cooked great meals. She was also a good friend to my dad.

Chapter 5

Baking Day

Although I loved our new house, I missed the people in my old neighborhood because I knew which days they baked, and oh how I loved to help sample their cookies. One of my neighbors dubbed me her *official cookie tester* because she could always depend on me to be there when the cookies came out of the oven.

Our washing machine was in the basement so one warm summer day while Hazel was busy doing laundry, I decided to visit our old neighborhood. After all, Monday was always cookie baking day.

I knew how to get downtown since it was only a few blocks away from our new house and I had walked that way many times with Hazel. Crossing the busy downtown street was going to be a problem though. For one thing, I was only three years old and wasn't allowed to cross on my own.

I stood at the corner stoplight debating what to do when suddenly, "Are you lost, little girl?" a nice lady asked me.

I shook my head and pointed to the other side of the busy street.

"I need to cross the street, but I'm not allowed to do it by myself," I said.

"I'll help you, the kind lady said. She took my hand and helped me get across. "Where is your mother, honey?"

"Oh, she's at the shoe store across the street," I lied. Once I crossed the street, I thanked the lady and made a beeline to the shoe store, pretending I was meeting up with my mother.

When I thought the lady was no longer watching me, I ran back out to the sidewalk and around the buildings on the other side of downtown. Once out of sight, I slowed down and took in the sights of the old neighborhood.

A couple of blocks later, I walked past our church and paused to look at it. We hadn't been to church since mom passed away and I missed being there. My mom had been the pianist there at one time; long before Danny and I were born. It seemed strange to be on this side of town all by myself. I decided to move on if I was going to complete my mission and be home before dark.

Suddenly I caught a whiff of something wonderful and I remembered why I was on this journey! I continued walking until I was closer tour old neighborhood.

I knocked on Mrs. Wilson's door. "Hello Mrs. Wilson," I said. "How are you today? Are you baking cookies?"

Mrs. Wilson smiled when she saw me and said, "Well, hello Elaine, I thought your family moved to the other side of town. What are you doing here? You're a long way from home."

"I just thought I would come and visit you."

"Honey, does your daddy know where you are?" asked Mrs. Wilson.

"Daddy is at work and Hazel was busy so I just thought I would come and see if you needed any help baking your cookies."

Meanwhile, back at home, Hazel realized I was nowhere to be found and was frantically trying to find me! The boys were still in school, so they were unable to help her look for me. She ran from one neighbor's house to another to see if anyone had seen me. She checked the corner grocery store, the school, talked to the milkman, the mailman, and every other person she could think of, and finally called the police.

***

"Well, good-bye Mrs. Wilson," I said. "I'd better go home. Thank you for the cookies!"

"Elaine, maybe I should call Hazel and let her know where you are."

"No, she won't be worried," I said.

I saw Mrs. Wilson pick up the phone to dial my number and then hung the phone back on the cradle when nobody answered at my house.

I walked a little further and knocked on another neighbor's door.

"Hello Mrs. Aho, how are you today? Did you just bake cookies?"

"Why, yes I did, Elaine. Would you like one?"

"Wait a minute. I thought your family moved to the other side of town. Do they know where you are?"

"Sure they do. I told them I was going visiting. Well, thanks for the cookies. I'd better get home now." She gave me another cookie for the road and I was on my way.

"I'm going to call Hazel and let her know you were here," she called after me. Once again, no answer at home. (No such things as answering machines yet.)

By this time, I was getting pretty tired and I still had to walk a good mile to get back home. I walked past our old house and then over to the elementary school so I could see our favorite big old pine trees one more time before I had to get home. I sat down under the large pine boughs, finished my cookie, and lay down for a rest before my journey. The scent of pine, the warm sun and the soft needles under the tree made me want to close my eyes and go to sleep. And that's just what I did.

From a distance, I hear someone calling my name, but I thought I was dreaming. Slowly I opened my eyes and saw a man in a uniform standing over me.

"Elaine."

I had been sleeping so soundly that I was having trouble focusing on the man calling my name. "Is your name Elaine?" he asked.

It was a police officer. At first I was a little scared because I couldn't remember where I was. I must have been sleeping really hard.

"Yes?" I answered.

"Little lady, you have half the town looking for you. How did you get all the way over to this side of town?"

"I walked," I said. "I missed my old neighbors and I knew this was baking day so I thought it would be a good time to go visiting."

"Well, I'm going to take you home now. Everyone is worried sick about you."

"Am I going to be in trouble?" I asked the officer.

"I guess that will be up to your daddy, but yes, what you did was wrong. I'm sure your daddy is very worried about you."

The police officer picked me up and put me in his squad car to take me home. He was surprised my little legs would carry me so far. I guess he didn't understand the power of freshly baked cookies.

***

"Oh! Elaine, where have you been?" Hazel cried as she wrapped her arms around me. "I was so worried about you!"

"We found her sleeping under a pine tree at the school over on the east side," said the officer.

"The east side, officer? Why, that's over a mile from here. How did she get there?" Hazel asked.

"I walked," I said. "I needed to make sure our old neighbors were still baking cookies on Mondays. Remember? I'm the official cookie tester."

When Dad came home, he was NOT happy after Hazel told him what had happened.

"Don't you EVER do that again, Elaine! What if you had gotten lost? We may never have found you!"

"I wasn't lost, Daddy; I was just following my nose."

Chapter 6

A Small Town

Life in a small town has always suited me well. Later in life we moved to St. Paul and lived in the suburbs; a place that I never felt comfortable, even though we were really still out in the country surrounded by farms.

In a small town, people thought nothing of allowing their kids to be outdoors with the supervision of the older siblings. Everyone knew people in the neighborhood and watched over one another's children,

***

"Oh no! I'm all out of baking soda," Hazel announced. "How can I finish baking these cookies without baking soda? I can't leave what I'm doing, and the boys aren't around to run to the store for me." The oven was on and she didn't want to leave it unattended while she ran to the store. She didn't want to turn the oven *off* because she would have to start her baking all over again.

In most every small town there were little mom and pop corner grocery stores on every third block or so where people could go for staples such as milk, bread, and other supplies. They also had a great candy and ice cream selection that you could get for as little as a penny a piece or less. Generally, people lived in the back or above the store and would come out front to wait on customers with the ring of a bell as customers entered the store. I always thought this looked like a nice, low stress way to make a living.

We had one of these wonderful stores right across the street from us.

On this particular day, their customer would be a little three-year-old.

"I can go to the store for you, Hazel," I announced.

Hazel looked at me long and hard before she finally decided maybe I could do this.

"Okay, if you think you'll be all right. Be SURE to watch for cars and look both ways before you cross the street," she said. "I'll be watching for you."

"I need a box of baking soda. Here is some money to pay for it; I'll write down what I need, and you can give the note to Mrs. Carboni."

"I can remember, Hazel; I don't need a note," I said.

"Ok, but go straight to the store and come straight home."

She put the note around the money just in case, and stuck it in an envelope for safe keeping.

She reluctantly walked me to the curb and watched me get safely across the quiet street.

"Baking soda, baking soda, baking soda," I said under my breath so I would not forget what I was supposed to buy.

"Baking soda, baking soda," I opened the door and heard the familiar tinkle of the bell."

"Well, hello little lady. What are you doing here all by yourself?" Mrs. Carboni asked.

"I would like a box of baking soda, please," I said.

"Well, aren't you a big girl coming to the store all by yourself," said Mrs. Carboni.

"Yes, I need some baking soda for Hazel."

"Are you sure it wasn't baking powder?" She asked.

I gave her a blank look. I didn't know two cooking things could sound so much alike.

"I'm sure she said soda," I said, feeling a little bit uncertain.

"Do you want me to call her and find out?"

"Um…" I said as I reached in my pocket for the money.

I reached in my pocket and pulled out the envelope and gave it to Mrs. Carboni. When she opened it, she found a small note from Hazel saying that she was sending me to the store for a box of baking soda.

"Well, Elaine, you were absolutely right! You ARE here for baking soda."

I breathed a sigh of relief.

With that, she rang it up, gave me the change from twenty-five cents and said, "You are a very big girl to be able to do this all by yourself."

"Now be careful crossing the street. I'll watch to make sure you're alright."

"I'll be careful, Mrs. Carboni. I'll look to the right and to the left before I cross the street."

When I got home, Hazel was waiting for me.

"I was really worried about you after you left. You're awfully young to go on such a journey. I really should not have sent you. We should have gone together."

"I was fine though, and Mrs. Carboni said I did a really good job!"

Chapter 7

Winter Wonderland

When we were kids, winter in northern Minnesota was nothing like it is now.

We had SNOW!

The adults generally cursed the huge amounts of snow but to kids it was pure heaven! Piles and piles of it that made for wonderful sledding and snowshoeing! The ice rinks and lakes were frozen as hard as a rock; perfect for skating.

We loved skating and playing on frozen lakes, but it meant waiting until Dad said the ice was thick enough to support us. Every day we would take an ax and a ruler and process to the lake to see if the ice was ready for us. Dad wouldn't give us permission to go out on the ice until we could prove that it was a good four inches thick. David, being the oldest, got to chop the hole and Danny would carry the ruler to see how thick the ice was. I just went along for the chance to be outside with my brothers.

"Only two inches," Danny sighed. "Look, there's kids skating over there - why can't we go?"

"Dad's just being careful," David said. "He would feel awful if one of us fell through the ice."

The three of us walked back home; our disappointment showing.

The next day we were sure we would be able to go out on the ice since the weather had dipped to minus twenty degrees overnight.

"Yeah! Five inches!" proclaimed Danny.

We ran back to the house to get even more clothes on and for the boys to get their skates. I didn't know how to skate yet but had a lot of fun pulling and pushing the boys across the ice and sliding with my boots.

***

We had great hockey teams throughout the Iron Range because that's what kids did all winter, but not on groomed ice arenas where ice time needed to be scheduled in order to go practice. They practiced out in the icy streets, stopping only to allow a car to pass. It was like the winter version of baseball. Just find enough kids for a good block and pass on both sides and you had a game. The rest of the kids would magically show up with their skates on, ready to go, as soon as they saw someone was playing in the streets.

***

Royal would have made a wonderful father for some kid, but it never happened. We were his kids. When we went to their house over Christmas break, we could see that he had spent days piling up snow in the back yard each time he shoveled the patio and walkway. This created a wonderful mountain of snow that we could play on. Best of all, we spent days jumping on it to pack it down and then digging to create a wonderful carved igloo with doors and windows to go in and out of. By the end of the week it was glorious!

The iron ore dumps across the highway made for great sledding because they were fairly steep, and the runs were long. We piled snow around fallen logs to make challenging jumps.

Sleds were wooden with steel runners that required waxing. They were heavy and required frequent rests on our way back to the top of the hill. Toboggans required the help of an adult to pull them - or several kids. They were lots of fun but *really* heavy!

With luck we could find a big piece of cardboard to slide on. It was lightweight, easy to carry up and down the hill and if you wanted to go *really* fast, you could go home and find some canning wax and wax it up really well. Then it flew! Sometimes cardboard caused some nasty injuries just because we went so fast.

I didn't have a sled yet, so Royal went to the local hardware store to get one for me. When he came home with my new toy, I was so excited! At last, my very own sled!

And then I saw what he had bought for me.

It wasn't a shiny new wooden sled with runners, it was about the size of my body and made of bright red plastic! I could barely hide my disappointment when I saw my new sled.

"Thank you, Royal; it's very nice," I said.

But Royal could see that I was disappointed.

"Something wrong, Honey?" He asked.

"It's just that I've never seen a sled like this before. It's not made of wood and doesn't have any runners. It's different from everyone else's and I'm afraid they'll all laugh at me," I said, trying not to cry.

"But *those* sleds are heavy, and hard to get up the hills. Once they see how light yours is and that you can go up and down the hill three times before they make it back up the hill once, they'll all want one."

Royal was very smart when it came to practical things and I knew he would never let me fail, so I thought I would give the new sled a try.

"How about if the four of us go up to the hill together and I'll make sure nobody laughs at your new sled," Royal said.

I agreed and we all set off for the "dumps."

An older bully called out, "Hey, where did you find the red chunk of plastic? Is that supposed to be a sled?" The other bullies laughed along with him.

I gave Royal a look of *you promised not to let them tease me.*

"Don't laugh until you see this in action," Royal said and smiled derisively to the boys.

We got to the top of the hill and Royal took me to a place that wasn't too steep for starters.

"Let's start here until we see how fast this thing goes," he said.

He gave a little push to get me started and I went down the small hill at a pretty good clip.

I got off the sled at the bottom of the hill and waived back at Royal with a big smile on my face.

I picked up my sled and ran back to the top of the hill for another try.

Kids with their heavy wooden sleds trudged up the hill like plow horses pulling their heavy load. They all stopped and looked at me as I ran by them with my shiney red sled tucked under my arms.

I quickly got to the top of the hill and was ready for another run.

Again, Royal gave me a push and down I went!

I picked up my little red sled and ran back to the top. Royal asked, "Are you ready for something steeper?"

"You bet I am!" I said, smiling.

David and Danny came over and asked if they could try my sled and I proudly said they could.

"You can use my sled for a while if you want," offered Danny.

"No thanks," I said. "I really like my own sled."

Royal smiled at me.

The bully had been watching me go up and down, up and down the hill while he trudged and panted between each run.

"Hey," he said as he collapsed in the snow, gasping for air. "Where *did* you get that sled anyway? I've never seen one like it but it sure looks easier than these things," he said as he pointed to his heavy, red sled.

"Ask my uncle. He bought it for me." With that, I gave Royal a big hug.

"Thank you for being so smart. I'm sorry I was being selfish. I love my new sled!"

Royal just smiled.

Chapter 8

The House of Wonder

Grandma and Grandpa Frank lived in a two-story house in Chisholm. It was white with an enclosed porch on the front which had two big old leather rocking chairs where we could sit and rock and watch the world go by. The front of the house was adorned with beautiful flower beds. The back yard was filled with a large vegetable garden and raspberry patch. Grandma canned everything her lovely garden produced in preparation for winter.

Both grandparents came directly from Finland in order to avoid further persecution from the Russians and Swedes and to find a better life for themselves.

Grandma was, for all intense and purpose, a mail-order bride. Grandpa knew her as a little girl growing up in their village. When he moved to America, he kept track of how old she was, and when she was sixteen, he wrote to my great grandmother and asked her if she would allow him to marry her daughter. If she agreed, he promised to send the money for the boat ticket to America. Grandma was terrified when her mother told her that she was to go to America and marry someone she had never met.

Leaving Finland would mean never seeing her family again as they would never have enough money for the trip across the ocean.

Poor Grandma! She loved her family very much and she cried and cried at the thought of leaving them. She begged her mother not to send her away, but her mother said it would be a wonderful opportunity for her. Life in Finland was becoming more difficult with each passing year. People were starving and villages were frequently under attack by the Russian armies.

After much deliberation and many tears, it was finally decided that Grandma would go but only if Grandpa agreed to pay for her sister to go as well. He did, and they both set off for America.

My grandparents were married shortly after Grandma got to the United States. By this time, she was eighteen and he was thirty-five.

When Grandpa arrived in Chisholm, he went to work in the iron mines as did many others who came to the Iron Range from Finland and other countries.

The work was hard and there were few regulations or concerns for the safety of the miners. Men were often sent into the mines with several sticks of dynamite and not enough instruction on how to use them. Sadly, the miners often didn't come home at the end of their shifts. The miners had to pay for all their supplies; shovels, dynamite, picks, lanterns and the candles that kept them lit, so they didn't earn much money for such hard work. Eventually Grandpa was fortunate enough to get a job manning the pump house for the Mahoning mine.

Because this area of northern Minnesota is quite boggy, it was important that the pumps ran around the clock in order to keep the mines from filling with water. His job was to keep watch over these pumps so the miners didn't drown or the mines cave in.

Eventually it was decided that it was more efficient to strip mine the ore by cutting large swaths of earth from above ground rather than digging into the ground by way of tunnels.

This eliminated the need for a pump house and a pump house keeper. Since the houses were destined to be torn down, the mining company offered the employees the chance to buy the pump houses at a minimal cost. Perhaps just for the price of moving the house to a new location.

Thus, Grandma and Grandpa had a very modest but nice two-story home.

***

Because we never understood the Finnish language, communication with Grandma and Grandpa was difficult at best. Nevertheless, we loved visiting our grandparents. Besides the fact that they were very sweet, loving people, there were always fun places to explore inside the house and out. An added bonus was that Grandma was a really good cook!

Our most intriguing place was the attic. It was a place that must have held many secrets because we were never allowed to go in there and snoop around. The thought of seeing this mysterious place made us all crazy with the anticipation of someday being able to explore the forbidden area.

When we visited our grandparents with Martha and Royal, we begged to go upstairs.

Martha could always find reasons for us NOT to do something. It was too cold up there. It was too hot up there. Surprisingly, we found out she was absolutely right once we were finally allowed to enter the mysterious room.

***

The three of us stood outside looking up at a window that was over the kitchen in an attempt to figure out what could possibly be upstairs.

"It looks like there's another room up there, like a bedroom or something," Danny said.

"I think it's probably part of the attic," David added.

"But look over here (we ran around to the other side of the house where there was another upstairs window). See? There are no curtains in that window and there are in the other one."

"Good point! This is getting really strange."

To get to the attic meant climbing an extremely narrow staircase which could best be described as a fat ladder with wide rungs. It took using both our hands and feet to get to the second floor in order to avoid losing our balance. Upon getting to the top rung, there was a trap door that could only be opened by an adult because it was heavy and long.

One day, the three of us decided to at least go upstairs and look at the room over the kitchen – just to see what it really was.

"Ok, but don't go inside the attic without someone with you," Martha warned.

What did *that* mean, we wondered?

What could possibly be in the attic that would require having another person with us?

We made it upstairs with some help from Royal who lifted the trap door.

Danny poked his head up first and looked around the room. From below, we imagined he must have looked like a gopher sticking his head up through a hole.

"You guys have got to see this! There's a really nice bedroom up here!

"I wonder why Grandma and Grandpa don't sleep up here instead of their own bedrooms," David said.

Grandma slept on the main floor in a bedroom with a double bed that was right off the dining room and separated by a heavy curtain.

Grandpa, however, slept on a very small, narrow cot under the attic stairway. It was very dark and foreboding and I wondered why he had to sleep there all by himself. I don't remember that Grandpa was ever well, so maybe this was easier for him.

During the winter months, Grandpa had to keep the wood burning furnace fed around the clock which meant he had to get up in the middle of the night to keep the house from getting too cold and the pipes from freezing.

The upstairs was unheated with the exception of an open vent that went to the upper level of the house to the bedroom. We thought it was great fun that we could sit at the grate and listen to all the adult talk going on below us. We would laugh and giggle as they carried on conversations. Their visits probably had nothing to do with us and were mostly spoken in Finnish, but we thought we were so clever that it made us giggle anyway.

We explored the hidden bedroom. It was bright and cheery with sunlight coming in. The rest of the house was fairly windowless because it made the house easier to heat during the cold Minnesota winters. The walls were a light green; the floor was decorated with rolled tar paper linoleum that was gray and printed with large feather plumes in shades of burgundy and white. It had nice lace curtains and a lovely bedroom set. It appeared to be a girls' room at one time because there was a nice comb, brush and mirror set. There were also girl-type things. It seemed odd to me that there was a picture of Dad on the wall, but the boys didn't seem to notice. They were too fixed on the attic door.

We bounced and rolled on the bed – quietly so we didn't get yelled at – and then straightened the covers again so nobody would know we were goofing around up there.

Then we all sat down on the floor and stared at the attic door as if willing it to open on its own. The door was just off the secret bedroom and had a HUGE heavy wooden door and enormous hinges.

"Whoa!" Dan exclaimed. "That door looks like it belongs on a dungeon! It's even bigger than a barn door!"

What in the world could possibly be in there that needed such a large door for protection, we all wondered?

"Don't go in there unless someone is with you." That was what Martha said. What did that mean?? What kind of secrets could possibly be in there?

David was looking intently at the walls of the bedroom and turned to take in the entire area. "The attic room has got to be huge. If you look at the house from up here, you can see that this room takes up a very small part of the upstairs."

David was very smart and had a tendency to think mathematically so his mind was telling him approximately how large the room was going to be. Danny and I just wanted to get inside.

Finally, we went downstairs to beg one more time to go into the attic and see what was there.

Royal was always willing to help us get ourselves in trouble so he said that he would go up there with us.

Giggling with anticipation, we carefully climbed the stairs. We walked through the bedroom and then Royal grabbed the huge handle of the monstrous sized door. It let out a loud, low groan that seemed befitting of such a beast. The massive hinges creaked under the weight of the door.

As the door slowly opened, we were hit directly in the face by a hot blast of pine scent as if the beast itself had spewed its pine sap on us - and we liked it! The summer heat warmed the attic so much, it literally took our breath away. We soon got used to it and were able to breathe normally.

I inhaled a deep breath through my nose. "Oooo! I *love* that smell!"

It took a minute for our eyes to adjust to the dark. Royal found a bare bulb light hanging from the ceiling by a single antique electrical cord in the middle of the room and pulled the metal chain to turn it on.

"Whoa!" We all sighed under our breath as we slowly turned around to see what was in the room.

"This place is HUGE!" Danny exclaimed.

The room *was* huge. It was a big, unfinished room with nothing but wood planks covering the studs. There was no insulation and no way of letting the heat out with the exception of a single window that stood about a foot above the floor. We opened the window to let some of the stifling warm air out and the fresh air in. Because it was a two-story house, the attic went straight up to the peak of the roof. One side of the room was built up and had a large loft that was built over the upstairs bedroom. There was a ladder that went up to the loft so we all scrambled up to see what was there. Grandpa had built a railing across the open area so people wouldn't fall to the lower level.

Back in the corners we discovered old steamer trunks and suitcases that were used by my grandparents when they came over from Finland. I know that because they were covered with stickers that had Finnish writing and the white and blue Finnish flag. They were amazing! Upon opening them, we saw a little closet area to hang suits and dresses. On the other side of the trunk were little drawers for small items and large drawers for bigger items. We pretended we were boarding a ship and drug our luggage around so we could go find our berth and set sail to America! We spent hours playing *immigrant* and took turns as the ticket taker and the bell hop. We set up a place to eat and had our pretend dinner together.

"Royal, we need to get home and get these kids to bed," my aunt said called up the stairs in her creaky little high-pitched voice.

"Ohhhhh," we sighed collectively. "We haven't even finished exploring."

"Maybe next time," Royal said. We all trudged down the stairs.

"Did you close the window? We don't want any bugs or bats to get in."

"I'll get it," David said as he scrambled back up the ladder.

He closed the window and then pushed the big heavy door closed with all his might. "See you later," he whispered to the attic as he pushed the latch closed.

"Martha, since you and Royal are coming back in the morning anyway, how about if Danny and I stay here with Grandma and Grandpa? It will give us some more time to spend with them," David suggested.

It was true. We had never had an opportunity to spend the night with our grandparents because we couldn't understand one another. Somehow, through the use of sign language along with the ten or fifteen words they had managed to learn in the forty years they had lived in the United States, we managed to communicate. They lived in a Finnish neighborhood, had Finnish neighbors, went to Finnish church, read Finnish magazines and newspapers, and they always had Martha nearby to interpret for them. Learning English simply had not been a priority.

"Where will you sleep?"

"In the room upstairs! It's a big enough bed for both of us."

"Me too!" I said hopefully.

"No, you're too little. Besides the bed is only big enough for two and we don't want you to sleep with us," Danny said.

I felt very left out on this little plan. Sometimes it's hard to be the youngest.

"Well, I guess it would be okay," Martha said. "Let me ask Ma and see if she is okay with this."

The boys were shocked that Martha agreed to let them stay! Surely she could have found *some* reason to say "No."

Grandma was more than happy to let me stay. I slept with her in her big fluffy double bed. It was the best slumber party ever – even if we still had to go to sleep at our normal bedtime!

The next day we had a wonderful breakfast of eggs, bacon, and toasted homemade wheat bread with homemade jelly. It was fabulous!

After breakfast, Grandma and Grandpa wanted us to help pick blueberries. We could tell that's what they wanted because they gave us each a little bucket that they had made from a used tin coffee can with a piece of wire fashioned into a handle. We set out for the field in the back yard.

Wild blueberries are abundant in northern Minnesota and Grandma and Martha took advantage of this as often as possible. Behind the house was a meadow of about twelve acres of nothing but wild blueberries and the occasional wildlife. The field was surrounded by pine trees so it was a beautiful scene. We picked and ate as much as we could before returning to the house. I never liked this job because it either required sitting on the ground while milking the berries of their branches or bending over and picking. I preferred to sit but it meant I was right in the middle of the bugs and spiders. I have never been a fan of spiders. The end result of this job, however, was some of the most delicious blueberry pie you could ever imagine!

When Martha and Royal came back the next day, we were happy to see them and tell them all about our morning.

"Can we go explore the attic again, Royal?" Danny asked.

"Sure, just as soon as I finish a cup of coffee and some breakfast."

"We waited patiently for Royal as he ate; v-e-r-y s-l-o-w-l-y. It took him forever! It was like waiting to open presents on Christmas Day.

"I would love some more coffee if there is any," Royal said to Grandma with a wry smile.

We all groaned and sat back, knowing it was going to be a while before we could go upstairs again.

His eyes twinkled as he took his sweet time drinking that coffee too just to watch our anticipation a little longer.

Finally, Royal finished his coffee and we ran to the steps waiting for him to open the door at the top of the stairs.

"You boys didn't make your bed. You need to do that before I let you into the attic."

They quickly jumped into action and the bed was made and looked good as new.

"Your mom wouldn't want you leaving her bedroom a mess."

***

I stood frozen at what I had just heard.
Wait! (I thought).
This was Mom's bedroom?
Nobody ever mentioned that.
This was *my mother's* bedroom!
I stood in the middle of the room looking at it with new, transfixed eyes as the boys and Royal went off to explore the attic some more.

This explained the "girl stuff" in the room. Why did I just assume this was Martha's old room? She was sixteen years older than Mom – of course this would have been Mom's room. She was the last one home as a young girl.

I laid face down on the bed hoping to catch her scent, but it smelled like boys.

I moved to the foot of the bed and lay on the bedspread because the boys hadn't touched that part of the bed. No matter how hard I tried, it just smelled like warm pine.

Her scent was gone. My eyes began to well with tears. I was so young when she left us that I just wanted *something* to hold on to that was hers. Something she touched. Something that was part of her. Of who she was.

I was four years old and couldn't remember anything about my mother. I missed the memory of her.

"Elaine, aren't you coming?"

"I'll be there in a minute."

I quietly went to the vanity and sat on the bench looking at myself in the mirror to see if I bore any resemblance to my Mom. People tell me that I look just like her, but I have Dad's blue eyes and light brown hair so I always thought I looked more like him.

Slowly I opened the drawers to see if there was anything left in them.

I let out a little gasp when I discovered that this part of the room remained untouched from when she left home to go to college. The drawer contained her nylon stockings and a few other under items. I touched them all knowing that at one time she had touched them too. She had worn these.

Her brush still had a few hairs in it, so I pulled them out and stuck them in my pocket. Later that day I carefully wrapped the hairs in a cloth handkerchief so I could pull them out of my pocket on occasion to look at them.

Other parts of the bedroom were adorned with awards from high school. Writings submitted to the school newspaper, music awards for choir and band competitions, a newspaper clipping announcing her engagement to my dad. That explained why his picture was up on her wall.

Her closets were empty. She had taken all of her things with her after she left home to go to school at St. Cloud Teacher's College and then to her first teaching job up in Ironwood, Michigan.

Although the room felt empty and alone, I somehow sensed her presence as I sat quietly and took in the entire room wall by wall.

This was my mother's room.

Her room.

***

"Come on Elaine! We found some stuff you'll really like!" David called.

I said a quiet good-by to Mom's room, wiped the tears from my eyes and ran to the attic to see what the boys were up to.

"Where have you been?" asked Danny. We've been waiting and waiting for you."

"Oh, I just needed to use the bathroom. What did you find?"

The boys handed me an old cigar box. I opened it. I wasn't sure what I was seeing at first but then Royal said it was my mom's little doll house.

There it was!

Something of hers!

She had carefully made little rooms in the box and little rugs to go on the floors. The furniture was all made of cast iron and everything opened and closed on tiny little hinges. The living room furniture was made of wicker in little miniature designs. There was a tiny hand-sized doll made of porcelain with metal hinges for legs and arms. Although she had been well loved and her face was a bit dirty, the doll was still beautiful! Best of all, it was Mom's when she was about my age. I played with it for a long time before I heard David say, "Whoa! What is that?"

In the middle of the floor there was a tower which we somehow had ignored when we first walked in. It was about 6 feet x 6 feet, stood about six feet tall and had woven rugs around the sides hanging from the top of the tower. What a perfect fort!

We looked under the rugs to see what was at the bottom of the tower. It was all blankets and more rugs.

"Hey, we could jump down from the top to the blankets," David asked.

"Sounds like fun!" Royal said. Just don't get hurt or I'll be in big trouble."

We loved Royal. He always let us play on the edge of doing something wrong.

Martha was always very strict and when she would catch us in the act of doing whatever she didn't think we should be doing, she would discipline us with a stern talk and a time out. Royal would sidle up next to us after she left the room and quietly ask in a silly little voice, "But did you have fun?" It always made me giggle. I always remembered that phrase and promised I would use it on my own children someday. It always made everything better.

We jumped and leaped all day. Who could have known a pile of rugs and blankets could have provided so much fun for us. By the time were called downstairs for lunch, three sweaty, red-faces little kids came downstairs, inhaled their repast and headed up the stairs to play some more.

"What in the world are those kids doing up there?" Martha asked.

"Having a blast," Royal said with a grin.

"Just having a blast."

***

We always thought Grandma's attic was the best; and that the basement was nothing more than an old cellar. We had never gone downstairs except to fetch something from the old pantry so Grandma wouldn't have to go up and down the stairs. We always grabbed what we needed and dashed back upstairs before the basement trolls got us.

One night, however, Martha called Grandpa and asked him to warm up the sauna because we were coming over.

"What's a sauna?" David asked.

"It's like a steam bath," Martha explained. You're gonna' love it!"

***Now, as a Finlander, I need to take this moment to explain that these should not be referred to as a "*saw-nuh*" as most Americans like to say. It's a "*sow-nuh*!" They originated in Finland and should be pronounced correctly.

***

We got to Grandma and Grandpa's, changed into our swimming suits, and went downstairs to the creepy basement, wandering the narrow wooden hallway to the sauna room.

We could smell the sweet, hot cedar scent as we got closer to the room that was waiting for our new adventure! Mmmm.

Martha opened the door and the heat from the small, wood paneled room nearly took our breath away.

The floor was covered by a raised wood sub-floor and bounced ever so slightly when we walked on it. The walls and floor were made of cedar to avoid rotting in high temperatures and this added to the wonderful aroma of warm wood.

There was a small stove in the corner of the room. It had rocks on top and the steam was wafting up from them. Next to the stove was a bucket of water with a ladle inside.

Across from the stove was a 3-tiered bench. "Just sit on the bottom bench for now. We'll see how much heat you can handle," Martha said.

We all sat like birds on a wire.

"What do we do now?" asked Danny.

"Now we sit here and get really warm. This is a different way to take a bath.

Are you ready for more heat?" Martha asked.

"Sure!" We all said excitedly.

Martha leaned over and picked up the ladle from the bucket of water. "Here we go!"

With that, she poured the water over the rocks. *TSCHSSSS! TSCHSSSS!*

The rocks protested against the sudden cold and belched out a cloud of steam. We all squealed with delight and even Martha giggled as the steam and the temperature rose even higher.

"It's getting *really* warm in here now!" David declared with a smile.

Our faces began to redden, and salty sweat poured down into our eyes. It was great!

"Can we go up to the next level?" Danny asked.

"You can if the heat isn't too much for you," Martha said.

We all scampered up to the next row. The sweat began to pour off of us and the heat was literally taking our breath away. We decided maybe the lower level was good enough and we all moved back down.

We wanted to take turns making the rocks send plumes of steam up toward the ceiling.

"Just a little at a time or we won't be able to stand it in here. The hot rocks are what make it steamy in here," Martha warned.

I got to go first - TSCHSSS!

Then Dan - TSCHSSS!

And finally, David - TSCHSSS!

With each small addition of water, the room became hotter and hotter.

"Now rub your skin hard and all the old dead skin will roll right off of you."

"This is so neat!" Danny declared as his skin rolled away.

"Will it hurt us?" I asked.

"No, this is why saunas are good for you. They do a deep cleanse on your skin and make you squeaky clean," Martha explained. "Are you ready to get out?"

"Yeah, it's getting really hot in here," we all agreed.

"Ok, let me go get some cold water and we'll cool down."

When Martha returned, we all went into an adjoining room and she poured the freezing cold water over our heads.

We began to emit steam from our bodies just like the old stove did when we poured the water on the rocks. We all giggled and squealed at the sight of ourselves steaming!

"Hey, this doesn't even feel cold!" David said in disbelief.

"Can we do this again tomorrow, Martha?" asked Danny.

"Well, maybe next week."

"Thanks, this was so fun!"

Grandpa came downstairs to shut down the fire and we all went upstairs to put our pajamas on.

We told Grandma all about our new experiences; we were so excited!! She didn't know exactly what we were saying but could tell by our expressions and excited chatter that we had had a wonderful time!

Grandma and Grandpa just smiled.

It was time to go back to Martha and Royal's in Hibbing. We got in the car, hugged and kissed Grandma and Grandpa good-bye and were on our way. We were all fast asleep in the back seat before we were out of town.

It was a good day.

Chapter 9

Daisy Bay Landing

As we got older, the boys and I visited Martha and Royal each summer for a week or two until we became too busy with events back home. David and Danny had paper routes so they were not able to come with us as often as they would have liked. I was six when I went up to Hibbing by myself to spend a couple of weeks with them.

That year Royal bought a speedboat before I arrived and they also rented a cabin at *Daisy Bay Landing* on Lake Vermilion! I recently spoke with the current owners of the resort and they have since changed the name to *Daisy Bay Resort*.

"Just so we're clear, I will never tow you behind this boat. No water skiing. This is for fishing and cruising and that's all," Royal said.

Royal was seldom stern with us so I knew he meant business. I was fine with that and jumped into the boat just to get the feel of it.

The next day we packed up, hooked the boat to the back of the car and headed on our long, 50-mile journey to the town of Tower and Lake Vermilion. The ride up there seemed to take forever!

Although not particularly deep (about 74 feet in the deepest part), the lake is huge! About 40,000 acres with 365 islands to navigate.

We jumped out of the car, checked in at the office and headed off to cabin #4. It was a neat little place that was right on the water and we were able to dock the boat right outside the front of the cabin. We could practically jump into the lake from the upper balcony (which Martha said would not be a good idea).

Since the boys weren't with me, I had to find my own fun. I quickly discovered the chipmunks outside the cabin were tame and would jump right into my hand for food, so I had all the entertainment I needed!

The water was a little too cold for swimming so that wasn't an option for me.

There were always fun things to discover at the shoreline. There were minnows to catch, hair snakes to untangle, swarms of baby bullheads to chase, crayfish to catch and snails to play with. There were also some of the largest leeches I have ever seen! I quickly got out of the lake whenever I spotted one.

Most of our days were spent fishing.

There are many bays on Lake Vermilion that present some interesting fishing experiences.

Being novice boat people, we spent way too much time trying to unhook our lines on the many dead heads in the bays. (Dead heads are old trees and branches that have submerged to the bottom of the lake.)

"Snag!" We would announce as Royal patiently backed the boat up to untangle the line. "Snag." "Snag." This went on for a very long time until we decided to find a new bay with fewer dead trees at the bottom of the lake.

We were just about to find a new spot when "Snag." I called out. But something felt differently about this one, "No, wait! I think it's a fish!"

"No, it's a snag," Martha said in disgust (never wanting to be wrong).

"No, it feels like a fish!" I said.

This argument went on like this until finally Royal intervened and said, "Oh my gosh, she's right – it's a big northern!"

He helped me set the hook so I could battle the monster right up to the boat. With Royal's coaching I reeled and fed it more line, reeled and fed it until it was almost up to the boat. The big fish dove back down to the bottom of the bay and I was sure I was going to lose it. He was not about to be caught! Finally, the fish was beginning to tire and so was I, but I managed to get him up to the boat. Royal reached a net into the water and helped me get the fish in. I was so excited! "See, I knew it was a fish!"

Martha was not happy to have been wrong and sulked all the way back to the cabin while I chattered non-stop about my new-found prowess as a mighty fisherman.

"Fisher *woman*." Martha corrected. Always the schoolteacher.

We continued to fish throughout the day, but the fish had finished biting.

What *was* biting, however, were the sand flies! They were ravenous and I provided them with a good target. Finally, I couldn't take it any longer and jumped over the side of the boat and into the water!

Martha was in full blown panic but Royal just sat and laughed. I had a life jacket on so I was perfectly safe.

"I think that's our cue to go home," Royal said. "Besides, I have a northern to clean and fry up for supper."

I was proud to have been able to provide the main course for the upcoming meal.

***

The next year, Danny was able to come with us. Grandma came as well since Grandpa had passed away and Martha didn't want to leave her home alone.

"You're gonna' love this place!" I told Danny as I told him all about the fun things there was to do (especially the chipmunks). We checked into a slightly larger cabin this time since there were five of us. It was a funny looking little cabin; really a small trailer with the side cut off and more rooms built on to the side of the trailer. We thought it looked like a great idea and called it "the cab-ler." (as in cabin- trailer.)

Fishing was always great on this trip! We always had plenty of fish for supper, and Martha and Grandma brought delicious vegetable dishes to go with them.

Evenings can get very cool when you're that far north, so we had our *Bemidji Woolen* coats and wool blankets along to keep us warm when we fished in the evening.

We discovered there was a wonderful sauna at the resort!

"Can we take a sauna, Martha? Please?" we begged.

She finally relented. "Oh alright, only one time though and don't stay in the water too long because it's getting pretty cold. And remember, *only once*!"

Royal was put in charge of watching us.

Back in Finland and other places north (Minnesota, Wisconsin, Michigan and into Canada), people who live on the lake tend a large hole in the ice all winter long so they can jump in after a hot sauna.

It was plenty cold late in the evenings, but fortunately it was July and there was no ice on the lake.

Danny and I got ourselves good and hot and then ran as fast as we could and jumped off the end of the dock into the frigid water! Our bodies steaming, we swam back and forth until we were starting to feel the cold from the lake.

We got out of the water, grabbed our towels and wrapped ourselves against the cool air.

"Could we do it one more time Royal? Please?"

"Martha said you could only go in one time. Are you trying to get me in trouble?"

"Who knows when we'll ever get to take a sauna again? Pleeeeease Royal?" Danny pleaded.

Royal stood up from his chair, peered over his shoulder at the cabin and whispered, "I don't see her. Go ahead, but I didn't tell you this was okay if she asks."

We ran back to the sauna, got good and hot, ran back to the lake and jumped in.

About that time, some fishermen were coming into shore. They were bundled in wool jackets, blankets and stocking caps.

"Are you kids crazy? This water is freezing!"

"We just took a hot sauna! We hardly even feel it!"

***

"Royal! Did you say they could go back in the sauna?" Martha yelled. "I specifically told them they couldn't do that!" Oooo was she mad!

"I told you we would all be in trouble," Royal said with a mischievous giggle.

"But Royal, we *really* had fun!" Danny said with a grin.

Royal smiled and we all went in to the cab-ler to get our tongue lashing from Martha.

Chapter 10

Night crawling!

The soil up in Hibbing is some of the richest, blackest soil you could ever imagine. Because of that, things grow to huge proportions. One summer I met up with the boys at Martha and Royal's. They were talking about all the things they had done and mentioned night crawling.

"What are you talking about?" I asked. "What's night crawling?"

"*You* don't know what night crawling is?" Danny asked as though *everybody* knew the answer to that. How stupid could his little sister be anyway?

Martha came to my rescue and explained, "Night crawling is where we wet down the garden just before nightfall. Once it's dark, we take flashlights out into the garden and shine in on the ground to see the night crawlers.

"Oh, okay," I said with some skepticism.

"Trust us," David said. "It's really amazing."

Now I had done my share of fishing and knew what night crawlers looked like, but I would hardly call them amazing.

It was something new to do so I agreed to try it and went out to help prepare the garden for the big event. I kind of thought maybe this was one of those jokes on the little sister but I went along with it.

Since Martha was all in favor of this, I thought maybe there was something to this story that I didn't know since I couldn't ever imagine her playing a joke on someone.

We all put our shoes on, doused ourselves in bug spray, grabbed our flashlights and went outside.

"Okay, when I say, '*go,*' shine your flashlight on one spot in the garden and don't move it," Martha said.

"Ready, set, go!"

Five flashlights came on all at once and things the size of garter snakes disappeared into the ground so fast, I wasn't even sure I had actually seen them!

"Wait a minute," I said laughing. "Was that a snake or a worm?"

"No," said Martha, "that was a night crawler."

"Holy cow, I've never seen anything move so fast! Let's try it again," I said.

Martha, Royal and we three kids tiptoed to a new location, counted to three and shined our light in new positions all over the yard watching these sleek speed demons.

I have never seen anything move so fast ever since our night crawling adventure.

Chapter 11

Leaving For Home

Work in the Iron Mines in Hibbing and Chisholm was slowing down so jobs were getting scarce up north. Natural resources only last for so long and once they're used up, they're gone. Dad had moved prior to the boys' finishing school in Chisholm, and Hazel stayed with the boys. He moved to the small town of Cohasset outside of Grand Rapids, Minnesota, because work was still available in that area. He found a place in the woods on the edge of Bass Lake where he built a wood platform, set up a campsite, and lived in his tent until he could find better living conditions for him and the boys. I think if it had been up to Dad, he would have lived that way until winter set in. Dad loved the out-of-doors.

It was decided that I should spend my kindergarten year with my aunt Charlotte and uncle Stan in Little Falls. This was fine with me as I knew they were very kind people who loved the outdoors. They had recently decided to build a cabin just north of

Little Falls on Fishtrap Lake in Cushing, MN and that sounded like great fun!

I went to live with them in the summertime as soon as the boys were out of school.

Since both of them worked during the day, the question became what to do with Elaine while we're working?

The solution was to have me stay with my Grandma Brunet (Dad's mother; Stan's sister) who lived upstairs from Charlotte's cousin.

Talk about good news, bad news!

The GREAT news was that Charlotte's cousin and her husband lived on a farm along with their three daughters, Joanne, Joyce and Shirley. Since I loved ALL animals, this was going to be amazing! There were cats, dogs, cows, chickens, pigs, and assorted other wildlife! I thought I was in heaven!

The bad news was that Grandma didn't like dirty, messy little kids. Especially little girls. I had never really met Grandma before, and I wasn't sure I was going to like spending so much time with her because I had heard she was very strict.

When we finally met, I *really* wasn't sure I was going to like her. She smiled at adults but not at kids. Her arms were always tightly crossed and she didn't really talk *to* you as much as *at* you. And then it was *not* to exchange pleasantries.

***

Every Easter, *The Wizard of Oz* was shown on TV for some reason. It was scary beyond belief and every kid loved it! The really disturbing fact for me was that I discovered Grandma bore a striking resemblance to the Wicked Witch of the West! Add some green paint to her face, cross her arms and it was almost uncanny! Except for the nose. Grandma's nose didn't look anything like the Wicked Witch's. Neither did her chin. It took me a long time to get over how much they looked alike and I would catch myself staring at her trying to imagine what she would look like if her face were green.

It was a little confusing to live with someone else. Everything was different; food, how to dress, how to behave.

Where Martha was always saying, "Flush the toilet!" Grandma Brunet would reprimand me for flushing every time. "Stop using so much water!" She would call out every time we used the bathroom. We were on a septic system and had to conserve water so as not to overload the tank.

It was pretty clear Grandma was not fond of little kids. She raised her own five and I think she felt that was enough! It took a long time before I saw a smile cross her face when dealing with me. It was always "don't touch this" and "stay away from that" and her favorite, "don't get dirty!" Was she kidding? It was a farm!

The girls downstairs took me in as a little sister and I loved spending time with them. We went out every day and slopped the pigs (that means we fed slop

– or wet grain – to them), fed the chickens and brought the fresh eggs in for Hildur (the girls' mom).

At night, we fed the pigs again and went out to find the cows and bring them home for milking. Sometimes they were far away in another pasture and we had a nice long hike to get them. The dogs would leap up from wherever they were napping and come running when we called out, "Let's go get the cows!" Even though one of the dogs was getting on in years, they would both scamper beside us like young pups, excited to be able to come along. They were amazing cattle dogs who loved their jobs on the farm.

The oldest dog was named Brownie for obvious reasons. A collie mix of some sort; serious about herding which was his instinct and he was good at it. Buster was a sweet lab/collie mix – maybe. All love and play; but not the brightest of dogs. Brownie would discipline him when necessary and was turning Buster into a herd dog in spite of his hunting instinct.

Hildur always treated me like one of the family and came to refer to me as her "other daughter." I liked that.

Joanne was four years older than me and the youngest of the three daughters. We have remained very good friends our entire lives.

Chapter 12

Life on the Farm

Even though I was five years old, my grandmother thought I should still be taking a nap. I think it was just to keep me out of her hair and also out of the barn. It had been at least two years since I had a nap and I wasn't willing to start taking them again.

Like all houses in this era, Hallberg's house was not air conditioned and summers were always hot and humid, so the thought of having to sleep upstairs in the daytime was unbearable! Joanne came up with a plan! "How about if Elaine takes her nap downstairs today where it's cooler?" she asked my grandma.

Grandma raised her eyebrow and looked at us with a certain lack of trust. "Well, I guess that would be alright – just make sure she sleeps!'

"Oh, we will."

***

Of course, we had no intention of my taking a nap so we had to devise a plan to get out to the barn without Grandma seeing us.

There were only two entrances to the house; the front door (where Grandma was sure to see us even from upstairs) and the back door. The back door would have been ideal because we could run straight to the woods, circle back, sneak behind the garage and the grain bin and straight to the barn! The problem was, in order to get to the Hallberg's back door, we had to go through the downstairs bedroom, past the stairway to Grandma's apartment first, tip toe through the back porch and quietly make our way out the back door. It would be risky. The hallway echoed loudly every time the door opened, and we knew she would be waiting for us to make our move so I could get out of a nap.

Hildur didn't think crawling out the window was a good idea although she thought it was funny that we were trying to sneak out. She was wonderfully good-natured woman who was always on our side. Besides, she knew five-year-old kids didn't take naps. On the other hand, she didn't want to lie to my grandmother either.

Only one thing to do. Recruit Joyce.

When Joyce went to the stairs leading to Grandma's, we followed behind her so we could dash through to the back porch while she talked to Grandma.

"Elaine!" Grandma yelled from upstairs as she jerked the door open hoping to catch me not napping.

(What, was she sitting on a chair next to the stairway waiting to hear me leave the house? Where was the trust?)

"No, it's Joyce." (We sneaked past her before Grandma opened her door). "I was just wondering if you needed some eggs."

Like two shadows we sneaked out the door, ran to the woods and doubled back trying not to laugh as we were running as fast as we could pump our legs. We were like Olympic athletes running from the Wicked Witch of the North! We were reveling in our successful plan and whispered how great we were to one another when from the upstairs bedroom window Grandma yelled, "ELAINE! You get up here!"

We stopped in our tracks. Joanne looked at me sympathetically. "Well, we tried our best."

"But we had fun," I said.

…...Busted.

I didn't think Grandma would yell at Joanne too, but she did. She even told Hildur what we had done!

Grounded for the day. What to do now.....

I sat staring out the front window for the rest of the day, watching the goings on down below in the farmyard and not being able to do a thing about it. Night finally came and I was able to fall asleep.

***

There was one big pig on the farm who was born a runt and had been raised from a bottle. To look at her you would never know that she didn't weigh 10 pounds when she was born – she grew up to be one whopping big pig!

"Here comes old Lou-Lou looking for her share of slop," Joyce said as the pig came running toward us. "No wonder she's so big – she's always the first one to the trough."

"Yeah, but you've got to admit she is a sweetie," Joanie added as she scratched the pig between the ears until the pig looked up at her with a smile on her silly face.

"Lucky for us she isn't mean, or she would be attacking us!"

"She's so tame I'll bet Elaine could ride her."

"Yeah, Elaine, why don't you ride her?" said Joyce.

Not knowing that this could possibly be dangerous, I climbed on the sow's back and rode her around the pen once she finished eating. The pig acted as though this was a perfectly normal thing to do so it became my daily routine.

Because pigs are generally the dirtiest animals on the farm, Grandma was not going to be happy....

Needless to say, I was one stinky mess by the end of the day.

Hildur burst out laughing when she saw me and said, "Boy, will your grandma ever be mad when she sees you!"

She came up with a plan in order to keep me in Grandma's good graces. "I'll see if you can take a bath down here with the girls and wash your clothes tomorrow. Maybe she won't notice."

"Thanks a lot," I said. "I must smell really bad for you to want to help me out."

Hildur went up to talk to Grandma and came back with my pajamas.

"Wow, she agreed to let us do this?"

We all took turns using the tub. It was decided I should go last since I was the dirtiest and then Hildur could wash my long hair so I would be good as new when I went up to go to bed.

She was great!

***

Life on the farm also taught me that not all animals are fun to be around.

On Saturdays, Hildur went to the Farmer's Market to sell or buy things from farmers and townspeople. One day she returned from the market with a couple of big gray geese that were not to be messed with. She adored them and they loved her back. Nobody else could get near them and I was an easy target being practically as tall as they were.

"Where are those stupid things?" I asked Joanie. "I need to get home for dinner."

She peered over the barn door to see if she could see them. "I think you're safe if you make a run for it. I don't see them."

"Okay, will you help me if they come after me?"

"Hmm, probably not. They hate me too."

"OK, here I go." I ran as fast as my feet would carry me, but the farmyard was sandy - I mean really sandy – like about eight inches of fine sand all over, so it was hard to get enough traction to run without falling down. I had run about ten feet when I got bogged down and fell face first. I looked up and saw the two geese running straight at me with their wings outspread, their heads down, hissing at me with their beaks open, ready to attack! They meant business! I tried to get up but continued to slip in the sand. One of them reached out and bit me hard in the leg while the other tried to bite as well. I cried and started to scream for help. I rolled up in a ball and kicked at them whenever they got near me so I wouldn't fall victim to their beaks any worse than I already had.

Suddenly, out of nowhere, Hildur came running toward me. With broom in hand, she batted at the geese and yelled, "You get out of here!" She swung the broom at them, so they took off running for about three feet and then casually waddled away, satisfied that they had won battle with the little kid.

I got up and ran all the way home, tears streaming down my face, welts and bruises beginning to appear.

"Grandma, I hate those stupid geese. Why did Hildur get them anyway?"

"Well, she likes them. I think they're her pets."

"Why couldn't she have just gotten a puppy?"

"When you go out tomorrow, just call me and I'll come out to protect you."

***

The next day as I was leaving the house, I looked in all directions for the geese. They were nowhere to be seen. I tiptoed quietly around the corner and there they were. Hoping they didn't see me; I ran back to the house to get Grandma as planned.

She grabbed a metal bucket and said, "Okay, let's go – I'm right behind you."

"But what if they bite you too?"

"I'm bigger than they are, and I have a bucket – I don't think they'll bother me." She didn't say that they would want to go after me first, but I knew that was the case, so I stayed close beside her.

No sooner had the words come out of Grandma's mouth when one of the geese ran at her from around the other side of the house! It had her dress in its beak and was pulling hard. Grandma swung her bucket around, caught the goose in the chest and sent it flying. The other one came running at her with its head down, beak open and hissing at the two of us. Grandma threw the bucket over the gooses head and yelled at me from over her shoulder, "Run! Get to the barn!"

I ran for all I was worth and made it safely.

I yelled back, "Thanks Grandma! I made it!"

When I turned to tell her I was okay, I actually saw her laughing! I began to see a slightly softer side of Grandma from that day on. We were *the goose team*! She and her pail protected me every time I went outside and we laughed at our conquests.

The following summer when I returned to Little Falls, the geese were nowhere to be found.

I hope they tasted good.

***

It was early July when Dad and the boys came down to Little Falls from their new home in Cohasset to visit for a few days. I was SO excited at the thought of seeing my family!

When they arrived at the farm, I showed the boys everything I knew about farm life while Dad visited with Grandma. Joanne was the same age as Dan, and Joyce was the same as David, so we all had a great time.

July was a time of parades and celebrating. We spent the weekend at the cabin with Charlotte and Stan, swimming, flying around the lake in Stan's new red, white and black *Falls Flyer* speedboat, catching fish, eating and watching fireworks.

On the farm, July meant getting the next cutting of hay bailed and into the hay loft in preparation for winter. The boys were able to provide the extra muscle needed to get this job done. I followed behind the hay wagon since it was too crowded for me to be up with everyone else. Since I was following far enough back to avoid getting dust in my eyes, I discovered a whole new animal world that was lying beneath the rows of hay. Sadly, there were more animals than I cared to see that were unable to get away from the big tractor and the jaws of the baler. The aftermath was a gruesome sight. This mostly included more mice, snakes and frogs than I had ever seen before!

As I chased the mice that had managed to escape back and forth from hay pile to hay pile, Joanne called out, "What are you doing back there?"

"I'm catching mice for the cats!"

"So are you going to carry them all the way back to the barn in your hands?"

I hadn't thought of that. I had a few of them stuffed in my pockets but they escaped as fast as I could catch them. I decided to let my catch go and find a box for the next trip back to the field so I could put the mice in it.

We put the first load of bales in the hay loft and I went about finding my mouse container.

When we returned to the hay field for the next load, I grabbed several mice and stuck them in the box. Joanne and Danny decided this looked like fun and joined in the great mouse hunt. We ran from row to row catching as many mice as we could.

When we got back to the barn, we collected all the bedraggled barn cats and set them down in front of the box. I pulled one mouse from the box and set it in front of them. The mouse froze in place debating whether to run or just die of fright and get it over with. The cats looked at the scared little mouse and slowly sauntered away. Some sat down and began cleaning themselves. Stupid cats! Here I just provided them with a smorgasbord and they refused to eat it.

I took the mice out in the pasture, away from the barn and let them go. Let the cats get their own food.

Chapter 13

Frogs

For some reason, every few years there was a huge army of frogs. Frogs so plentiful they could actually become a hazard.

While driving down the road at night, it wasn't uncommon to see a multitude of them hopping across the road at the same time. Since it was impossible to miss them, and it would take forever to wait for them all to cross the road; several of them were driven over and this caused the road to become very slippery!

Needless to say, frogs were everywhere!

I mentioned all the strange things I would see behind the hay baler and frogs were definitely among them. Sadly, many of them were badly maimed by the time we got to them.

David, Danny and the girls had devised a plan to help the injured reptiles and were very instrumental in trying to put the frogs back together.

In a book that David was never able to finish, he wrote the following entry:

"Many of the frogs were dead but others were missing a foot or a leg. We picked them up and stroked their heads to calm them as their sides heaved heavily with panicked breathing. Then Joyce said, 'Let's fix them up.' We all agreed and gathered up as many frogs as we could carry. I picked up some extra legs and feet in case we needed them.

Across the farmyard from the barn was an old ramshackle chicken coop that was no longer being used. The flat-topped wooden nesting boxes were far from sterile, but they were high enough to use as tables so we set up a surgery unit in the old coop.

We didn't have much to work with – string and strips of an old sheet. None of us had ever seen sutures, so we didn't think of using a needle and thread to close the frogs' wounds.

I ran up to Grandma's flat and asked her if I could borrow a bottle of iodine. She raised one eyebrow and looked at me with her sharp eyes. 'What are you going to do with it?' she asked. I told her we wanted to put it on a frog that had lost its leg. She looked at me for a long moment then stomped off to the bathroom and returned with a bottle of iodine. 'Don't use it all up,' she said.

I ran back to the chicken coop where we took turns painting iodine on the exposed flesh of split stomachs and footless stumps. One frog's leg had been severed below the joint, and the foot dangled by a piece of skin. I put the two halves of the leg back in contact with each other and tied a strip of cloth around the leg to hold the pieces in place.

Dan saw what I was doing. He took one of the spare feet and tied it to the leg of a frog that had lost its foot. We all caught the spirit and soon all the spare legs and feet were tied to frogs that needed them.

We put all the frogs in boxes and pails, then took one last look at them, wished them good night, and trooped out of the chicken coop.

God forgive us. We were young, and we had no practical knowledge or wisdom to match our enthusiasm for doing a good deed. Even if it didn't heal as good as new, a frog with a grafted limb, we thought, had to be better off than a frog with a stump. It only stood to reason.

In the morning, we ran to the chicken coop to visit our patients. I hope no doctor ever has to face the sight that greeted us. Nearly all of our patients had died during the night. Whether from the trauma of the mowing or from the trauma of our surgery, we couldn't tell. Perhaps they simply died of dehydration. Or perhaps the limbs we grafted onto their legs began to rot overnight and poisoned the patients.

We buried the frogs in a dirt pile behind the chicken coop. Then we all sat in the dirt in front of the coop, with long faces and tears in our eyes. We did not follow the tractor that day.

We had wanted to move the world, to rescue all the wounded animals but we lacked the wisdom to do it.

Nevertheless, the desire to do good has stayed with me all my life. We learned that day that good intentions are not enough to relieve pain and suffering. Wisdom and understanding are needed as well. Years later, Joyce studied to be a nurse, and I wonder whether it was because of the frog hospital. I've taken courses on CPR, so I would know what to do if someone should have a heart attack. Dan has spent a lifetime studying the body's natural healing process and is regarded by his friends as a healer.

Above all, I am still the one who follows the tractor trying to hold on to what I saw as a child. Not the carnage left behind but the nature of the soil, grasses, birds and frogs rather than taking the view from the tractor seat.

They were just a boxful of sick frogs, but I think they touched us more than we touched them. Forty years later I ran into Shirley at a funeral and she asked, 'Do you remember the frogs?'

"Yes, how could I forget?" David answered.

How could any of us forget?

Chapter 14

The Swimming Hole

Summers in Minnesota can be downright miserable with heat and humidity!

The six of us were out wandering in the fields on such a day when the boys spied a large, rectangular, man-made pond.

"Hey, I didn't know you guys had a swimming hole!" Danny said.

"Well, it's not really a swimming hole; the cows use it," one of the girls said.

"Oh, we don't mind sharing it with the cows," David said. "We just need to cool down."

They ran back to the house to tell Grandma they were going to go swimming and to get their trunks on.

"Just where do you plan on going swimming?" Grandma asked them with a scowl.

Grandma wasn't thrilled that they were going to one of the stock ponds to swim, but she knew they were both good swimmers and would probably be fine.

She must have though the boys were talking about a water trough though because *everybody* knows what happens in a stock pond. They ran back to the pond and jumped in! They ran and jumped and cannon balled and had a great old time. "Come on, girls! The water feels great!" Danny called.

"No thanks!" The girls giggled to one another. "You know you're swimming in a cow pond, right?" questioned Joyce.

"We don't care!" David said. "At least we're cooling off.

They continued laughing and having a great time as they swam and threw thick, black, smelly muck at one another and smeared it all over their bodies.

The girls sat watching them in disbelief. How could those silly boys not know what happens in a stock pond?

At last they came out of the water. Every pore in their body reeked of the muck in the pond.

"Boy did that ever feel good!" Danny announced.

"Pee-yew! You guys really stink! You should walk behind us so we don't have to smell you all the way home," Joanne said. "Your grandma is going to have a *fit* when you walk in the house. You might want to hose yourselves off and use *lots* of soap before you go upstairs."

As Danny turned to talk to the girls, he saw the cows heading toward the pond.

"Hey, look, the cows are going in for a dip now."

No sooner had the cows entered the water when they all lifted their tails to relieve themselves.

"Eww! I'm glad we aren't swimming in there now!"

The girls looked at each other and giggled knowing the truth behind the boy's swimming escapades.

"We told you the cows *go* in there," Shirley said.

***

The time came when the boys had to leave and go back up to Cohasset with Dad, and I was left behind with Grandma. I really hated to see them go but I knew there was no other choice. It was how things had to be for now. I often worried that I would never see them again.

Chapter 15

The New and Improved Grandma

Although she would never admit it, Grandma was finally beginning to enjoy the company of her new little roommate.

Every night she would read the new *Winnie the Pooh* adventure that was part of the funny page section of the daily paper. How I loved those stories! I would have her read them several times until I could practically recite them back to her. Finally she would smile and say, "Enough! Go to sleep!" She pretended to sound gruff but I could tell that there was a hint of smile in her voice and that she was beginning to enjoy our bedtime routine.

She also had a big book of nursery rhymes that she read to me until I could recite them all by heart. We would laugh reading them together every night.

Saturday mornings were special because I was able to listen to cartoons on the radio! No, really. Every Saturday there was radio theater that you could listen to and it was an exciting new adventure every week. I can't remember any of the stories now, but I do remember the music that began the program because it was *really scary!* It would start out with a bassoon playing a creeping up behind someone sort of song and then the man would come on and sing in a somewhat breathless voice;

> *"If you go down to the woods today*
> *You're sure of a big surprise.*
> *If you go down to the woods today,*
> *You'd better go in disguise!*
>
> *For every bear that ever there was*
> *Will gather there for certain,*
> *Because today's the day the*
> *Teddy Bears have their picnic."*

I kinda' let it slide that the song was about a teddy bear's picnic because the man did such a good job of making the song absolutely scary! The story would begin.

It was always a hair-raising adventure of some sort and there was a full cast of characters reading their scripts to me. I sat in front of the oversized radio and listened intently. By the time the story was over, I was sitting so close to the radio I had practically crawled inside it! Whew! It was *wonderful*!

I actually began to feel sorry for kids who had to watch cartoons on the television because they didn't get to use their imaginations.

Commercials were a welcome relief because they allowed me to catch my breath before the story began again. When the story was over, I always felt a bit of a letdown. It was a little like watching the closing number on the Mickey Mouse Club. I knew that the show would be back "real soon," but watching the sad faces of Cubby and Karen and rest of the Mouseketeers singing their good-byes always brought a lump to my throat.

I knew Grandma got a kick out of watching me because I would hear her talking to Charlotte over the phone and telling her all about me listening to the latest adventure.

She loved to see me bound across the room to the radio every Saturday when she would call, "Elaine, it's 9:00, time for your cartoon!"

Grandma smiled at me a lot more by now.

Chapter 16

A Weekend at the Cabin

We often went to the cabin on weekends and I loved it!

The cabin was a new structure that sat in a bay with a thick stand of cattails on one side and open water with a few reeds on the other. Stan and I would take the duck boat out into the lily pads across the bay and hunt for turtles. He taught me to put the net slowly *under* the turtles and quickly lift the net rather than trying to catch them by going over their heads. We were an amazing team! Once we caught all we could find for the afternoon, we would take them up to the cabin which sat on a long slope and let them all go at the same time. Everyone would choose a turtle or two and bet against each other to see whose turtle would make it to the lake first. Once they hit the water, we would guess to see which one would be the first to stick its head out of the water to catch a breath of air.

That summer, Stan taught me how to row the duck boat on my own. It was called "the duck boat" not because it looked like a duck, but because Stan had painted it in camouflage colors so he could take it out duck hunting in the fall. It was a small boat – about six feet long and four feet wide so it was quite buoyant, and Stan didn't worry about me tipping over. I spent hours rowing around in search of turtles. I practically lived in the boat and Stan eventually let me fish from it. A few years later, Stan would teach me to drive the motorboat and take it out on my own! It was like getting a license to drive at the age of 13! I was becoming an avid and savvy lake person! I spent the day in the boat, out in the reeds and fish for sunnies and crappies until late in the day, stopping only for meals.

But that was later in years. At this point in my life, I was only 6 years old and not ready to use the boat on my own yet.

I was growing up as an only child since the boys were with Dad and I was still dodging the welfare people.

Not having any siblings around made it difficult to find things to do while I stayed in a house full of adults. Stan was always good at teaching me about nature, feeding ducks, taming chipmunks, fishing ... but I didn't really have anyone to play in the water with. Surprisingly, living in northern Minnesota where most everyone had a lake cabin or at least spent time at the beach, very few adults actually knew how to swim so they were all reluctant to get in the water with me. Stan swam with me for a while, but he was a grownup. He didn't want to spend all his time with a little kid.

While the adults visited up by the cabin, I entertained myself by catching baby bullheads, crayfish and occasionally having to run up to the cabin to have a bloodsucker or two removed. Eww!

One day Stan brought out a couple of rubber inner tubes and I had a blast playing with them. Since I was not able to swim, it was fun to have this large tube to hold me up.

Back then, car tires all had a rubber inner tube inside (no radials yet). If you had a flat tire, you removed the tube, found out where the hole was, patched it and put it back inside the tire. Good as new! When there were more than a few patches per tire, you bought a new inner tube and gave the old ones to the kids to swim with.

The day was beautiful. The sun shone brightly and glistened off the lake. A slight breeze kept the air from being too warm and I was floating in my inner tube enjoying the day.

***

"Oh my gosh! I forgot about Elaine! Does anyone see her?" Charlotte asked, her voice full of panic.

"She was playing down by the lake last time I saw her," Grandma said; her voice rising in panic as well.

"Oh no, I don't see her anywhere!" All the adults ran down to the lake to see if I was still by the water. There was no sign of me.

Fearing the worst, Stan ran down by the dock; binoculars in hand. When I was still nowhere to be found, he jumped into the fishing boat to see if he could find me. Maybe I had drifted back behind the island.

I can only imagine the fear they were all experiencing as they searched high and low for a little girl in the water. Nobody wanted to say the word "drown" out- loud but you knew that's what they were thinking.

"What are we going to tell Paul?" asked Grandma.

"Let's not think the worst yet – she still may be safe on the water. It looks like she had the inner tube so maybe she floated out further into the lake."

"Oh, that poor little girl – she must be terrified!"

"Well, I don't hear any screaming or crying for whatever that's worth," Charlotte said.

Meanwhile, Stan was driving slowly up and down the shore in the fishing boat.

Suddenly, from across the bay, he yelled, "I found her! She's over here behind the cattails!"

Everyone cried in relief!

I had fallen asleep in the inner tube and drifted well into the reeds – sound sleep.

When Stan approached me with the boat, he was careful not to startle me so I wouldn't jump and fall through the hole in the inner tube. "Elaine," He said softly. Then a little louder, "Elaine." Finally, my eyes fluttered open and I jumped a bit when I discovered I was asleep on the water.

Stan gave me a rope to hang on to and pulled me back to the cabin.

I was safe with the exception of a bad sunburn; being a bit waterlogged and a few nasty horsefly bites.

I had never seen grownups cry happy tears before.

Chapter 17

The Bull

A large truck pulled into the farmyard one day and three men helped Bob unload a HUGE black and white bull!! It was far and away the largest, most ornery animal I had ever seen! The kind we would expect to see in a rodeo (if we had ever been to one). Not only was it very tall, but it was extremely muscular and had a face that forced you to look away every time he looked in your direction and let out a loud, low snort. We knew right away that this was not a bull we wanted to make friends with. I would definitely not be riding on *his* back around the pasture! He was terrifying.

It was several days before Bob finally put the bull out in the pasture with the rest of the cows. Prior to that, he had been in a corral in the barn, so that added to his already bad temper. When Bob let the bull go into the pasture, it ran and bucked at the notion of finally being free. The girls and I were worried about going into the same pasture to get the cows for fear that we would accidentally run into him with no place to hide.

"Daddy, we're not going anywhere near that bull. He's too scary and we're afraid he'll kill one of us if he catches up to us while we're getting the cows," said Joyce defiantly.

Bob was a tease and taunted us at the idea that we would be afraid of his little bull. 'Girls are afraid of bulls; girls are afraid of bulls," he sang.

Bob won, of course - the bull stayed in the pasture.

"So, what do we do if the bull charges?" Joanne asked the oldest sister Shirley as we walked through the barnyard gate to get the cows. As the oldest, we relied on Shirley for all the answers. She was our David.

"We should come up with a plan. Let's be sure to keep our eyes open for a way out at all times."

"Elaine, can you climb a fence?"

"Of course, I can," I answered.

"Then you and Joanne run to the woods and either jump the fence or roll under it as fast as you can. Joyce and I will run the other way."

"But you're running to an open field! You guys will be trampled!"

"We'll be okay. We'll have the dogs with us and they can distract the bull while we run. Besides there's two of them – they know what they're doing."

We walked slowly and carefully that evening looking right and left in case the bull appeared.

Normally we would be laughing and singing and having a great time as we walked along. This time we were quiet and on guard. We were relieved to find that there was no bull in sight that evening.

The next morning, he was out in the barnyard in all his stupendous glory – head held high, muscles bulging - glaring at us - daring us to come inside. He lowered he head and pawed at the ground as we walked by and we scooted away from the fence as fast as we could. I think he was laughing at our fear. We knew he could charge through the electric fence and not feel a thing through all of his muscle. We ran to the barn to get far away from him.

"Boy, I thought the geese were bad, but this guy really scares me!" I said.

"We just need to keep an eye out for him at all times," Joyce reminded us.

Evening came and it was time to get the cows again. The four of us, along with the dogs, walked quietly through the pasture; ever aware that the bull could be around the next tree. We were always on the lookout, watching for places where we could run to safety. We never made a sound as we walked. Even the dogs were on guard.

After a mile or so we saw the cows down in a valley and called to them, "Come boss, come boss."

No bull in sight.

Slowly the cows lifted their heads and began to move in our direction lazily swinging their heads back and forth, grabbing mouthfuls of grass and leaves as they walked. They plodded along the well-worn path to the barn so they could be milked for the evening before we turned them out to pasture again.

"Hmm, no sign of the bull," Shirley said quietly while looking carefully all around her. "Maybe he got out and ran away."

I had noticed a very strange anomaly and stopped to watch it for a few seconds.

Shirley came up behind me and asked what I was looking at so intently.

"Well, it's the strangest thing. Look over at those lilac bushes. Every now and then a big cloud of dust will appear out of nowhere from behind the bushes and sails straight up in the air. I'm trying to figure out what would cause that?"

"Where?" Shirley asked.

"Right over there behind those tall bushes. Watch, there'll be a big cloud of dust, then it stops, then another cloud. What do you suppose would cause that?"

We all stopped and watched this phenomenon for a second or two and almost laughed when it suddenly occurred to all of us what was causing the strange puffs of smoke.

"Run!" shouted Shirley.

We quickly realized that the bull was behind the bushes pawing at the ground and throwing dust high into the air, ready to charge! Suddenly, he burst through the bushes and ran straight for us!

Joanne and I ran toward the woods and threw ourselves under the barbed wire fence while Joyce and Shirley ran further behind us just as the bull began to charge! The dogs quickly jumped into action and began barking, nipping and running circles around the bull to get its attention away from us. Joyce and Shirley found a good place to get under the fence and dove to safety. In the meantime, the dogs were putting their lives on the line for us and continued to draw the bull away from our direction.

"What if he hurts one of the dogs?" I cried. Brownie was a determined and faithful old dog and I feared for his safety. With the bull bucking and throwing himself back and forth, his hooves were getting dangerously close to the dogs.

The dogs were amazing and worked tirelessly and in tandem to defend their family.

***

I once saw the two of them go after a badger while we were out haying and saw how they worked together to take down their prey. Pound for pound, badgers are one of the strongest and fiercest creatures in North America and Europe; but working together, the dogs took the angry varmint out in no time at all. As gruesome as it was to watch this attack, I couldn't help but feel a sense of pride at the kinship of those two dogs and seeing how they worked as a team.

***

The dogs lured the bull away from us and ran to the safety of the cornfield. Bulls are strong and fast, but because of their bulk and size, they don't have a lot of stamina when it comes to running. Eventually the bull gave up and trotted back to the barn.

Probably the scariest moment of my life!

We watched from the safety of the other side of the fence as the huge animal stared at us, head held high and snorting as though to say, "Just watch your backside girls. I'm coming after you."

***

Joyce was hopping mad at her dad as she told him what had happened to us. She was never afraid to speak her mind and we were all grateful for that. We all agreed it was not safe to be in the same pasture with that bull and refused to be with him ever again. Bob didn't believe the bull was that mean and teased that we were just being sissies. "Afraid of a little bull? Ha!"

***

The next afternoon we were walking to the barn to feed the pigs that were housed in the side barn when we heard Bob yelling and saw him running through the woods near the pasture as fast as he possibly could with the bull charging right behind him! I didn't know adults could run like that! His arms and legs were pumping as fast as they could while the bull lowered his massive head, bellowing and snorting as he ran toward Bob, gaining speed with every motion. Had it not been so serious, I would have laughed because he looked like a cartoon character with his legs running faster than the rest of his body.

Bob made it to the wall of the side barn and began frantically scrambling up the six-foot sides. He almost cleared the wall when the bull caught up to him. We all let out a scream, afraid that the bull would smash him into the wall and seriously injure him. The bull butted him with his massive head and sent poor Bob sailing up in the air and over the fence. His arms and legs swam through the air as he went over the fence and he had the "good fortune" of landing in a soft pile of manure on the other side which cushioned the fall.

From then on, the bull was chained up in the barn. I still wonder how they got the bull to agree to go in there.

Chapter 18

The Pig

I previously mentioned the side barn.

This was an addition to the original structure. It could be entered through a door from inside the barn and then jump down about two and a half feet to get down to the pig pens at ground level. (Or you could get thrown over a fence by an angry bull).

The side barn was divided into a series of farrowing pens and used for sows when giving birth to their piglets.

"You'd better stay up there in the barn," Joanne warned. "These sows can get pretty mean if they think you're going to bother their babies. Besides, you can watch them from the barn."

"The babies are adorable!" I said.

"Yeah, but don't come any closer."

"But what about you? Are you safe down there with the pigs?"

"I have food for them, so they're not really interested in me. The trick is to get in, feed 'em, and get out as fast as possible. You could hand me the slop pails and then I can get out of here, so I don't get bitten."

Hildur often helped with this job too. She didn't take any guff from those old sows and would give 'em "what for" if they tried to charge her or bite.

Pigs are very large animals with a serious set of jaws and incisors that are about an inch and a half long. They can do some serious injury to anyone who falls into their pen so I was always nervous watching Hildur and the girls do this chore. These pigs were nothing like Loo-Loo.

Bob bought a huge male pig and brought it home one day.

We girls looked at it with our mouths hanging open when we first saw it.

"They told me this pig has a temper so stay away from him, girls. Let your Ma feed him until he gets to know us a little better," Bob said. We were a little fearful for Hildur every time she went to feed the beast. She would kick at him when he got too close but that didn't deter him from coming after her.

Hildur was short but feisty! She could fight off the pig and leap into the safety of the barn faster than anyone I had ever seen!

One evening, Hildur said, "Bob, that pig is too dangerous to have around. He comes after me every time I get around him. I'm afraid someone's going to get hurt. I have to jump into the other pens to get away from him. Just get rid of him – I don't care what you do. It's not worth everyone's safety."

Bob let the conversation drop without a solution to the problem.

Late in the summer when the piglets are sold, the sows aren't as dangerous to be around. The girls were able to take over the pig feeding chores again. The old boar was put in a separate pen because he was not to be trusted. Joanne and I finished up the chores for the evening, fed the pigs, closed the barn door and left for the night.

***

The following morning, we entered the barn for our morning chores.

"Well, look who's here!" Joanne said.

The big old boar was lying in one of the stalls next to the bull, his hind quarters hanging in the gutter and his upper half in the stall. He raised his head when he saw us.

"What are you doing here? You're supposed to be in your own pen." She kicked at the pig to get him to stand up so she could get him back in the side barn. The pig let out a squeal, attempted to stand and fell back. "What's wrong with you? Get up, you stupid pig!"

"I don't understand why he won't get up. Give me a hand here, Elaine."

We shoved and rocked but the pig refused to move. He would get up on his front legs, squeal in protest and then fall back.

Joanne gasped, "I think his back legs are broken." What in the world happened here?"

We both looked up to see that the door to the side barn was standing wide open.

"You didn't close the door last night," Joanne said to me.

"Me? Are you sure you weren't the last one out?"

"No, I'm pretty sure it was you. You *always* need to close that door and this is why."

My stomach churned inside me. I didn't like the pig, but it was important to the family for breeding purposes. I thought I was going to throw up.

My mind raced to retrace my steps from the evening before when Joanne and I finished slopping the pigs. Did I really leave the door open? Was I the last one out? I really couldn't remember. I guess I'll never know.

"Don't tell Daddy or he'll be furious!" Joanne warned.

Furious? How could I not tell anyone what had happened?

Did I really do this? What if I was never allowed to come back to the farm?

We got Joyce to come and look at the pig and she thought that the pigs back legs were broken or that his back was paralyzed.

What do we do?

Our own crime scene investigation surmised that the pig somehow leaped the three feet up from the side barn, bumped into the bull in the dark and the bull kicked and stomped on him.

Poor pig!

We finally told Hildur what had happened, and she walked to the barn to look at the pig. No blame was made on either Joanne or me. It just happened.

And that's how Hildur told it to Bob.

I was sick to my stomach for days. I began having horribly sharp stomach pains, but I couldn't tell Grandma what was going on or she would tell Bob and Hildur the whole story, and Joanne and I would both be in trouble.

What should I do?

The pains continued to worsen.

I barely spoke for the rest of the week for fear I would burst into tears and would have to tell someone that I was to blame for the pig's condition. I still could not recall which of us left the door open.

By the end of the week the paralysis continued to move up to the pig's heart and he died.

Bob put a chain around the pig's legs and pulled him out to the barnyard with the tractor.

I'm not sure why it took him so long to call the rendering company to come and get the pig, or why he didn't just bury it, but it stayed in the middle of the hot barnyard, the pig's stench a constant reminder of my (?) failure.

Bob gathered us all together and told us how much that pig had cost him due to our negligence. When he finished reprimanding us, I ran upstairs and threw up.

Grandma came into the bathroom to find out what was wrong. I was sobbing uncontrollably and finally spilled the whole story to her. I told her I really didn't know who forgot to close the door, but "Please don't tell anyone else what happened." She agreed it would be our secret and gave me a hug. I felt better and eventually, over several days, my stomach pains began to subside.

Chapter 19

Agate hunters

The next weekend I was at the lake with Charlotte, Stan and Grandma.

There were no kids; so once again, I was busy finding my own entertainment.

"Why don't we go agate hunting," suggested Charlotte.

"That sounds like fun," I said, anxious to do most anything at this time. "What's an agate?"

"They're beautiful orange rocks with white and dark brown stripes in them. You'll love this," Charlotte said.

There are different types of agates throughout Minnesota, but they are not to be found everywhere. When polished, these rocks are absolutely beautiful. Some people cut them to show off the beautiful striations on the inside of the rock.

It just so happened that there was a huge band of agates throughout the Fishtrap Lake area.

We set out with small pails to put our rocks in and went in search of treasures.

Since the cabin had recently been built, the turned earth was able to produce several agates of various shapes and sizes. It was fun to compare the rocks and colors.

We spent several hours looking and comparing and were just about to break for supper when I saw it!

On the very lip of a precipice sat an agate the size of Stan's fist. The ground around it had slipped into a large, deep ravine, leaving the beautiful rock teetering on a throne of sand as though it wanted everyone to see its beauty.

I gasped. "Look!" I said. "It's huge!"

I held my breath as I cautiously crawled on my belly to the place where the rock teetered before falling into the ravine.

Slowly I reached my hand out and let it hover over the beautiful rock for a second before I lowered it like a crane and grasped the rock, bringing it back to me.

It was mine!

I opened my hand to see what I had found. It was beautiful with many colorful striations. I licked it to bring the stripes out.

"Look!" I said as I showed it off to everyone.

They all admired it sufficiently and then said, "Let's call it a day and go eat."

"Good idea!" I said. "We can look for more rocks tomorrow."

To this day, my family walks with their heads down in agate country, hoping to catch sight of an amazing find.

Years later I had the rock cut and polished and it still sits on my desk.

Chapter 20

Reunited

I enjoyed the rest of the year as a kindergarten student in Little Falls and lived full time with Charlotte and Stan.

It was early the following summer when Charlotte took the phone call from my dad.

They visited for a while and then I noticed her lips begin to quiver a bit and her eyes begin to well with tears. She turned her back to me and continued talking.

Eventually she put on a happy face for me and said, "Well, she's right here – you should tell her this news yourself. She handed me the phone. "It's your dad, Elaine."

She handed me the phone and then she walked upstairs so I couldn't see she was crying. Her hopes of permanently making me her daughter suddenly disappeared. Stan followed her up the stairs.

"Hi honey, how are you doing?" My dad asked.

I told Dad I was having a great time. I told him all about the adventures at the lake and the farm. Yes, I had loved kindergarten and had a nice graduation celebration.

"Well, I wanted to tell you that I got married and we would like you to come up to Cohasset to live with us."

I was a little confused.

"You got married? I didn't even know you had a girlfriend. Who is she?"

"Actually, you know her. It's Lorraine from Chisholm."

"You mean our neighbor?"

"Wow, that sounds great! I really like her. What about Gary and Nita?" I asked.

"We'll all live together and they will be your step brother and sister."

Step siblings weren't as common as they are today so this was a little confusing, but Dad assured me that we would all be fine.

"When will I come to live with you?"

"We'll come down in a couple of weeks to get you. That way you'll have time to pack your things up."

"What about Charlotte and Stan? I thought I was going to stay with them longer. I'll really miss them," I said with a lump in my throat.

"You'll see them soon. We'll get down to Little Falls often and you can spend some time with them in the summer months."

By now I had grown very fond of Charotte and Stan and knew I would miss them terribly.

***

A few weeks later, Dad and Lorraine came to pick me up along with David, Dan and my new siblings. Grandma came to say good-by as well. It was a very tearful ending to a wonderful saga, but we all promised we would see each other soon and that I could spend summers with them.

In spite of the fact that I was going to miss Charlotte, Stan and yes, even Grandma, this was going to be an amazing new adventure! I was finally going to be together with my dad and brothers, AND…my best friend from Chisholm was now my sister!

Life was pretty good right now.

Chapter 21

Life in the Woods

We were all together in Cohasset in our tiny 8 x 38 - foot trailer. Seven of us! We were very cozy to say the least. Our sleeping arrangements were a little tight and required some creativity! There was a fold out couch in what served as the living room which David and Danny used, Lorraine and Dad were in a small bedroom in the middle of the trailer, and Nita and I slept head to foot on the top bunk while Gary slept on the bottom bunk. When you're not very big to begin with, you don't realize how small a place is. It's just cozy.

We spent a lot of time outside as long as it wasn't raining or blizzarding and I am forever grateful for that. I learned a lot about the land, birds and animals, and respecting the environment.

David and Danny had lived up north in this quaint little trailer with Dad for about a year so they were very "woods savvy" by now and were excited to show me everything. What they were soon to find out is that I had come to be a bit spoiled living with older adults with no children of their own. I was used to getting my own way. I was a brat!

First, the boys showed me the swimming hole. We put on our swimsuits, grabbed our inner tubes and other swimming paraphernalia, and headed along the well-worn pathway through neck-high grass to the swimming hole.

The Bass Creek (we called it a crick for some reason) flowed out of Bass Lake, along a quiet little highway and under a large, round viaduct. It eventually became part of the Mississippi River a few miles down the channel.

The water that flowed from under the viaduct provided an endless source of entertainment. It began about ankle high but within two big steps it was knee high; then because the water flowed quite swiftly as it turned the corner from the viaduct, it dropped to well over our heads into a big pool and then returned to knee deep all within about fifty feet. We would wait and catch the water just right, lift our legs and let the water pull us along to the shallow end. Confident swimmers would let the current plunge them down and touch the bottom of the sandy pool before they were pulled to the shallows. If this wasn't timed just right, the current could cause some nasty nose scrapes. We never swam beyond the culvert because it was too unpredictable with an undertow that could take you all the way to the Mississippi.

There were lots of kids in the trailer court so we always had plenty of playmates.

I loved watching the kids swimming and splashing in the creek.

"Come on!" They would say to me. The water is great!"

The problem was that I couldn't swim.

Martha always filled my mind with, "Don't go in the water; you're gonna' drown!" And so I believed I would.

Danny was frustrated with me since I wouldn't just lift my feet and float. He did everything he could to get me in the stream.

"You're gonna' drown!" I couldn't get Martha out of my head.

How could I go swimming when Martha had already confirmed that I would, indeed, drown.

When we broke for lunch, Nita loaned me a small life jacket and helped me get into it. "Are you sure this will hold me?" I asked.

"You'll be perfectly safe. Here," she said. "Let's put my rubber dragon on you too; then you'll be extra safe."

She blew her dragon up for me. It was fun watching the little lump of colorful plastic take on life as she blew into it. First the head popped up as it filled with air, then the body began to take on shape. Eventually it was completely inflated. "Now step into this," she said.

"Are you sure I'll be safe?" I asked.

"Don't worry, you'll be fine."

We all went back to the swimming hole after a lunch of peanut butter and jelly sandwiches and orange Kool-Aid.

All the kids swam and laughed as I stood on the side of the stream and watched with a smile on my face. It looked like such fun!

"Come on!" Danny coached. "You'll be fine."

"But Martha said I would drown!" I protested.

"You have a lifejacket and a dragon! You'll be fine, now let go and swim! All you have to do is lift your legs and let the water take you."

I lined myself up with the stream in diving position, ready to let go at a moment's notice but I just couldn't lift my legs. It was as though they were frozen in place.

The words, "You're gonna' drown" kept going through my head like a mantra.

Finally all of the kids began chanting, "Swim, swim, swim, swim!"

I was holding all of them up for their turn to swim.

I held my stance at the mouth of the stream but my legs just wouldn't move with Martha chanting in my head, "drown, drown, drown, drown."

Danny had had enough of my nonsense. He came up behind me and gave me a little push. "Oops!"

"Ahhhhhhhh!" I screamed as I splashed into the water and began floating downstream. "Danny, why did you do that?" I yelled in fear.

And then I realized...I was floating!

I wasn't drowning, I was floating. And it was fun!

The day was coming to a close. The sun was beginning to go down so we had to get home for supper and be in the house before the mosquitos descended on us.

I so badly wanted to go down the stream again, but my legs refused to cooperate and let go. Martha was in my head again.

"We gotta' go!" David called to me.

"Can't I go one more time? Give me a push again."

It didn't happen. All the kids were on the trail ready to go home for supper. They were laughing and chattering and making plans for the next day and left me behind. I finally joined them because I didn't want to be out there all alone.

When we got home, I was in tears. I was frustrated with myself and mad at Martha.

"What's wrong, Elaine?" Lorraine asked.

"Oh, she's mad because she didn't get to go down the river one more time," Gary said.

"Well, why couldn't you wait for her to do that?" Lorraine asked.

"She's been standing there all day trying to go down but she kept saying Martha told her she was going to drown," Gary said.

Lorraine stifled a laugh.

"Well, that's what Martha always told me," I whined.

"Let's have some supper and you and I can go down to the crick and try it before it gets too dark," Lorraine said.

After supper I put my swimming suit on and Lorraine and I went back to the creek with Nita's life jacket and rubber dragon.

We were at the mouth of the pool when she leaned down and said, "Now sit back on my hands and relax."

I let out a little squeal of both excitement and fear. I clung to her arms for fear she would let go.

She laughed. "It's ok. The lifejacket will hold you. Even if the dragon loses air, the lifejacket will always hold you up. That's what it's meant to do," Lorraine said.

I finally relaxed and sat back on Lorraine's hands. "Now just lift your feet and let go."

"No, don't let go of me!" I said with panic in my voice.

"You'll be fine. You do want to learn how to go down the crick, don't you?" she asked.

"Yeah, but…"

"Yeah, but you'll be fine. Now lift your feet."

I did what she said and she gave me a gentle push. I began to bob my way down the stream. I squealed with delight! "I did it!!" I said. "I'm swimming!"

We tried it two or three more times until I could finally do it on my own.

I was SO excited I couldn't wait for Danny to see me go down the stream on my own the next day.

"We'd better get home fast or the mosquitos are going to eat us alive," Lorraine said.

We headed home as quickly as we could.

"Guess what!" I said as soon as I went got through the door. "I went down the crick all by myself!"

"Oh yeah, sure," my brothers taunted with grins on their faces.

"I did, didn't I, Lorraine?"

"Yes, she did. Just wait until you see her tomorrow."

That night I went to bed feeling a serious waive of accomplishment. I was both proud and excited. Lorraine tucked us all in for the night. When it was my turn I said, "Thanks for helping me swim, Lorraine. That was so fun!"

I gave her a serious look and asked, "What do you want me to call you anyway?"

"You can call me whatever you want," she said.

"Should I keep calling you Lorraine?"

"That would be fine," she said.

"It seems strange to call an adult by their first name. Could I call you mom? I've never called anyone 'Mom' before."

She looked at me with understanding and said, "I would like that."

I turned to my new sister and asked, "Nita, would it be alright if I called your mom, *Mom*?" I asked.

"Sure," she said. "I guess she's your mom now too."

And so it was.

I finally had a mom.

Chapter 22

The Big Beak!

When we had finished breakfast and were getting ready to go to the crick, I chattered away about my new accomplishment as though I had won the gold medal in swimming.

"You just went down the crick with a life jacket and dragon," Danny said. "No big deal."

"It is too a big deal, I'll show you!"

We got to the pathway with the tall grass and I took the lead. I couldn't wait to show everyone that I could swim now! I ran ahead of the group with wild abandon. I went over a small rise along the path and suddenly came face to face with a large, open beak!

I let out a blood curdling scream! A blue heron was coming slowly toward me with its neck extended, its huge beak wide open and its enormous wings spread out. I could see all the way down its throat! Its long legs taking slow, deliberate strides toward me. I was terrified! My legs spun in mid-air as I somehow managed to turn myself around without touching the ground and run back to where the kids were walking all in a row.

"What in the world are you screaming about!" Danny demanded.

I was white with fear, so they knew something bad had just happened.

I told him what I saw and that the bird was HUGE! At the time I was not the birder that I am today so I had no idea what kind it was although I knew I had seen them at the cabin.

"Oh, you're just making this up," Gary said.

No, it was huge! It was looking me right in the eye and it was coming at me with its mouth wide open!

"I think she's telling the truth," David said. "She looks like something *really* scared her."

We looked all around the area but didn't see any bird tracks or a break in the grass where he or she might have come through. It wasn't likely that a heron would be on a pathway since they are water birds, but I know what I saw.

From there I took my place in the safety of the middle of the line looking furtively to the right and left as I made my way along the path.

"Ok, wonder woman, let's see you swim," Nita said.

And I did.

Chapter 23

The Fishing Boat

As kids, we didn't realize we were poor. We had a baseball and bat, the boys had fishing poles and tackle (very important to our survival), everyone but me had a bike (but that was okay) and we had a deck of cards and a checkerboard. For the winter, we had skis and a sled or two that we all shared. If nothing else, there was always cardboard to slide on. We didn't need much more, because our life was outside no matter what the weather was.

The boys loved to fish and hunt and were very good at both, but mostly fishing.

Dad was very possessive of his boat, motor and gear so the boys mostly fished from the shore, casting their lines far out into the water. Sometimes they would load up their fishing gear and bike down the highway to the bridge that went over the Mississippi and fish from there as so many others did. Wherever they went, they always came home with supper.

"You know," said David, "we really should have a boat. It would make fishing so much easier."

"Yeah, good luck getting Dad to let us use his boat," Gary added.

"Why don't we just build one," said Danny.

"Great idea," David said. "Where do we find lumber?"

"Let's just go to the lumberyard and see if we can have their scrap pieces. Maybe we can find just what we need."

The boys borrowed a wagon and set off to the lumberyard to see what they could find. Their three best friends went along to help. The boys were always good at coming up with interesting things to do, so they never had any trouble getting kids to help.

"While we're walking, watch for nails so we can find enough to put the boat together," David said.

The six of them went off to the lumberyard to look for spare wood and nails in order to make their boat.

I'm sure they all had an idea how the boat would look when it was finished. In their minds it was going to be a beautiful masterpiece!

The boys came home hauling the weight of the lumber in their wagon and carrying everything else that didn't quite fit. They set to work sawing and hammering and straightening the nails they were able to find.

They had learned the importance of frugality from my father, but also from our grandfather. Grandpa would spend hours straightening used nails and fixing old pieces of wood to make them useable again.

***

When Grandpa tore down an old shed from behind the house, he spent hours sorting the wood and carefully pulling the old nails, trying not to bend them.

Royal showed up to see if he needed any help and found Grandpa straightening the nails one by one. He held them in his left hand with his pliers, and with the hammer in his right hand, he tapped away until the nails were as straight as he could possibly make them.

"What on earth are you doing, Victor?" Royal asked.

Grandpa smiled and held up a nail to show him how straight it was,

"Oh, for Pete's sake, why don't you just go and buy some new nails."

Grandpa wasn't sure what Royal was saying so he continued straightening the nails one by one.

In disgust, Royal got in his car and went to the local hardware store. When he returned, he handed Grandpa a paper bag. "Here!" He said as he handed a bag of new, oily smelling nails to Grandpa. "Use these."

Martha came out to see what was going on and Grandpa explained something to her that Martha had to interpret.

"What's he saying?" Royal asked.

Martha smiled and said, "He says these are too nice. He'll keep them for a special project."

"Ahhh! Stubborn old man," Royal said in disgust.

Grandpa carefully took the precious bag of new nails into the house. He came back outside and continued his mission of straightening nails.

Three years later old age and a hard life overtook my grandfather and he passed away.

While cleaning out his bedroom, Royal found the bag of brand-new nails tucked carefully in Grandpa's underwear drawer, still in their original paper bag.

Royal looked at the stash, shook his head and smiled. He carried the bag of nails downstairs and set them on the table in front of Martha.

"I guess he never found a project deserving of these nails."

***

The boys thought maybe they should have a plan for building their new boat.

Both David and Danny were good artists so they set about drawing what the boat should look like given the amount and size of lumber they had.

They spent days hammering and sawing.

"What in the word are those kids up to?" Dad asked Mom one evening.

"They're building a boat so they can go fishing. I don't suppose you could save them the trouble and let them use your boat."

"Absolutely not!" Dad said. I won't have them ruining my boat and motor."

The new boat was coming along nicely if the boys said so themselves.

"I wonder how we could get wood to bend?" Gary asked. "It would be nice to have a rounded bow rather than a square bow." Since there was no You Tube yet to show them how to bend wood, they had to settled for a square bow.

"Well, this is the best we can do given what we have to work with," David said.

The boys stood back admiring their work and contemplated their maiden voyage.

The boat was about four feet long and two feet wide. The bow was flat in front but I admired the fact that they got it to angle up so it gave the illusion of a very small barge. The front didn't exactly meet in a point but it wasn't bad. The bottom was perfectly flat so it was more of a raft with sides.

"Let's put it in the water and see if it floats!" Said one of their friends.

The boys all agreed and the boat was launched.

No sooner did it hit the water when it began leaking profusely from every seam.

"Whoa, pull'er up, pull'er up!" yelled David.

Everyone grabbed the boat and pulled it onto the shore.

"I think we need to find something to put in the seams to keep the water from coming in," Gary said.

The boys thought for a minute and then Danny came up with a brilliant idea.

"I know!" he said. "Grab some coffee cans and follow me."

The street department had recently been putting strips of tar in the cracks of the highways in preparation for the winter months ahead. It was just what the boys needed.

"Let's go get some, melt it down and use it to patch our cracks."

"Great idea, Danny!" one of the friends agreed.

They took off with their buckets.

When no cars were coming, they ran out into the quiet highway, pried up a line of tar and pulled until it all came off. They repeated this technique until they had enough tar for the boat. They ran back to where the building project was happening and melted the tar.

Next they smeared the sticky tar into the cracks with small pieces of wood and waited for it to set up.

Dad pulled up on his way home from work just as the boys were getting ready to launch their boat one more time.

"Hi boys, what are you up to?"

"Hi Dad," said David. "We just finished our boat. You can watch us launch it!"

"That's quite a boat guys," he said skeptically. "You've been working hard! Where did you get the tar to patch those seams?"

"Oh, we just found it," Danny said casually.

"Well, let's see if it floats," Dad said.

David, Dan, Gary and their friends all got into the tiny boat at the same time. The boys were all but sitting on top of each other in the narrow little boat when one of the friends said, "Maybe you three should go alone. It's your boat. We'll help push."

The tiny boat was launched, and the three boys stood with a look of excitement on their faces.

Suddenly, the boat began to rock back and forth throwing the boys to the bottom of the boat.

"I think we better sit down," David said.

They manned their handmade paddles to help steer, but without a rudder, the boat continued to rock back and forth, violently throwing the young boys from side to side. With a final heave and the boat tipped upside down, trapping the three boys underneath.

Dad jumped into the river to pull them out. They were all safe and sound.

"Boys, this is not going to work."

Dad thought for a moment before he carefully chose his words.

"I'll make you a deal. If you *promise* that you or your friends will NEVER use this boat again, I will let you, and you alone use my fishing boat but NOT the motor. You can use the oars and row wherever you want to go.

Did Dad really say that???

Nobody ever gets to use his boat the boys thought!

Their faces lit up and they promised that they would take extra good care of the boat and that no one else would be able to ride in it. AND they had to wear their life jackets at all times.

"It's a deal!" The boys all cheered.

The next day was spent taking the homemade boat apart and the boys decided to keep the wood for a future project.

I've always wanted to see the look on the street department workers' face when he went out to the highway, only to find that the tar that he had just laid the day before had suddenly disappeared!

Now that the homemade boat was taken apart and the wood safely stored for the next project, the boys were ready to take Dad's fishing boat out. They made sandwiches and grape Kool-Aid to take along on their fishing trip. They went out and dug up enough worms for an entire day, grabbed their fishing rods, tackle boxes and life jackets and were on their way.

They all walked a little taller that day because they were about to go out in a real fishing boat and catch supper for the family. It was up to them to prove to Dad that he could trust them with his prized possession.

Chapter 24

The Builders of Tall Towers

I don't know where the boys acquired their carpentry skills, but they all seemed to come by it naturally.

Our need to build forts helped us to achieve one of our finest feats ever!

While walking through a grassy, woodsy area near the trailer court, we came across a copse of four perfectly aligned aspen trees that just begged for a tree fort to be built right there.

"We should go get the lumber from the raft and a build a tree fort. Look, this place is perfect!" David said.

"Hey, you're right," Danny agreed. "We'll need some two by fours, plywood and nails to get this done. Now, in his adult life, Danny became a master carpenter who could build an entire gazebo with pegs and holes – no nails necessary. I guess it was his youth and the constant search for nails that helped him to become so adept at his skills. He also was an art major in college so he had an eye for things artistic as well.

The quest for supplies began as we all scattered with our building assignments.

The boys' best friends were Marv, Billy and Dale. Marvin's dad owned the trailer court so he had access to most of what we would need to build whatever they wanted to.

When the boys came back, they decided the first thing they needed was a ladder so they could get up to the platform.

Nita and I and a few of the other neighborhood girls, were the "go-fers" and handed the boys whatever they needed.

The platform was done. It was magnificent!

All ten of us scrambled up to the platform to happily survey everything around us from our new altitude. All except David. His eyes were on the trees above us and he said just one word. "Higher."

Once again, we set out for lumber and nails. Once again, we built another ladder and another platform.

"This is great!" Gary said. "Let's go look for stuff to put in it."

We came back with blankets, pillows and a toy telephone.

"What do we need toy telephone for?" asked Marv.

"In case we need to talk to each other," I said indignantly.

"Hey, I know," Nita said. "I have a great idea that I learned in school. I'll be right back."

She ran home in search of string and tin cans. Before leaving the house, she took a hammer and nail and put a small hole in the bottom of each of the cans. Next she took string, ran it through the holes, made a knot on each end and made sure she could pull the cans tightly without the string coming out.

She ran back to the tree fort and proudly announced, "Look, now we can really talk to each other with a real phone!"

Gary grabbed one end and ran up to the second story to check it out. "Hello?" he said. "I can't hear anything," he shouted down to Nita.

"We have to pull them tightly so the sound travels through the string. Make sure the string isn't touching anything."

Gary pulled the string tight. "Hello?" he said.

"Hey, I can hear you! This really works!" Nita exclaimed.

We all took turns with the phones and were amazed that sound could travel from two tin cans and some string.

"Okay, new rule," said Billy. Girls on the first floor, boys on the second floor.

"Oh, come on!" protested the girls.

We spent the day basking in all we could see from our new height. On occasion, the boys generously allowed Nita and me to go up to their floor for a visit. Especially if we went back to the house for a cookie run.

"Hey, maybe we could sleep out here tonight," Dale said.

"That would be fun," said Danny, "but the mosquitos would eat us alive."

We all agreed maybe that wasn't such a good idea.

***

For some reason the skunk population that year was terrible. We had to be very careful about where we were stepping to be sure we didn't surprise one while we were running through the tall grasses and weeds.

We decided that it would be a good idea to have "skunk scouts" in case one should be anywhere near the tree fort.

Nita and I were to be the scouts for the day. We wandered through the tall grass of the forest in search of skunks. When we didn't find one, we decided we should just have a pretend skunk alarm just like the fire drills in school.

We ran back to the fort yelling, "Skunk! Skunk!"

Everyone ran to the second floor because that's what we would do if there was a real skunk.

"Good job everyone!" David said. "Let's practice it one more time so we know exactly what to do."

The drill was repeated and we all felt quite confident that we would indeed survive a skunk attack.

David looked up at the trees though and said, "I think we should go up one level higher because a skunk really could spray us from here. And of course, there is the possibility of bears too."

Few of us had ever seen a bear in the area but we knew they were out there somewhere.

The sunlight was beginning to disappear so it would be time for supper and then the mosquitos; the third floor would have to wait until tomorrow. Besides, we needed more supplies for our new building project. We needed to scout the area tomorrow.

***

The next day everyone arrived with lumber, hammers, hand saws and nails. They were all ready to get started on level number 3.

We sawed and hammered and worked diligently all day until the next level was complete.

"This is amazing!" We all agreed, looking down from our new and higher vantage point. We all sat and smiled, enjoying the fruits of our labors.

"You know what? It's getting a little warm. What do you say we all go for a swim before it's time for supper?"

"Good idea, Marvin." We all agreed and headed home for our swimming suits and towels.

"Last one to the river's a rotten egg!"

***

We were hard at work on our building project early the next day since David convinced us we really should try and go for broke and make five stories.

"Hey, the trees are tall," he said. "Let's take advantage of it."

"That sounds really cool," said Billy, "but I don't know if these trees can hold that much weight – it's starting to sway a bit."

"Yeah and I can't get any more lumber from my dad," Dale said.

"Then we're just going to have to split up and find all the wood we can," said David.

By the time we hit three stories our phone system wasn't working as well as it did on two stories.

"HELLO?" We would shout.

"I CAN HEAR YOU. WHAT DO YOU WANT?"

I think our phone system had hit an early version of a dead zone.

***

Work continued on the fourth and fifth floors until at last, we were finished. We all had our doubts about going all the way up to the fifth floor since we could see it was really beginning to sway in the wind. Those brave enough to go up there were not feeling that this was a good idea but David convinced a couple of hearty souls to stay up at the top.

Nita and I decided three floors were enough and stayed where we felt safe.

We were thinking it was time for another skunk alarm. This time Gary and Billy went out to make sure the area was clear of the odiferous rodents.

While they were gone, the wind began to pick up and the sky was turning black.

David and Marv were up on the fifth floor when the trees really began to sway.

"I think we need to get down - *now*!"

"I think you're right, let's get out of here!" Marv agreed.

By now the tree fort was not only swaying but each individual tree was beginning to sway to its own rhythm and the fifth floor began to creak and groan. The wind was blowing fiercely and the rain was coming down hard.

"Get down fast!" said David.

Thunder cracked overhead and shook the entire fort! Lightning began to flash all around us. This was not a safe situation!

Those of us on the 3rd level were swaying back and forth so hard we could barely crawl to the ladder!

The fourth floor ladder broke apart leaving its inhabitants stranded.

"You're gonna' have to jump, David!" yelled Danny. "Try and swing your legs in this direction and we'll catch you."

They jumped safely down to the third floor and we all scrambled to the ground as large pieces of the fourth and fifth floor fell behind us. We ran as fast as we could to get out of the way of the flying debris.

Just as we finished a head count, the skies opened and the rains poured down on us. The wind practically whipped us off our feet as we all ran to the safety of our own homes.

The next day we went to see what had happened to our fort during the storm.

What remained was pure carnage. Boards dangled from various levels, swaying back and forth as though taunting us to try it again.

We all stood stunned looking at the mess and realized how unforgiving nature could be. We all could have all been seriously injured.

So, what are we going to do now, David?" one of the boys asked.

"I think we just pick up our mess and forget about the tree fort, he said."

It was a gallant effort on the part of all of us. We were proud to have been part of the project and to have been able to reach into the heavens. But we pushod the limits of the four trees that provided us with the fort to begin with and it was time to walk away.

Sometimes nature wins.

Chapter 25

The Campout

Dad came home from work one evening and said he had a surprise for us.

We couldn't wait to see what he had brought home because we seldom got presents.

"Go look in the back of the car."

We all ran to the car to see what he had stored in the trunk. We opened it up to find two orange, oily smelling lumps of canvas.

"What are these?" Nita asked.

"They're tents!" Dad exclaimed. "I got a good price on them at the Army Surplus store and thought you guys could have some fun with them."

Our faces lit up at the thought of our very own tents.

"Wow! Thanks Dad!"

We were all amazed that Dad had provided us with such a generous gift.

The tents were made of heavy canvas and were stored in canvas bags. Even though they were considered two-man pup tents, it took all five of us to lift just one of them from the back of the station wagon.

They were heavily oiled in order to make them waterproof. I'm pretty sure one wrongly placed lit match would cause them to burst into flames.

"Can we sleep in them tonight?" Gary asked with anticipation.

"I think we should set them up and let them air out for a day or two so they don't smell so bad," Dad suggested.

Dad showed us how to set up the first one and coached us through the second so we would know how to set them up on our own.

They were amazing; and even if they reeked of oil, we couldn't wait to use them.

We woke up bright and early and ran outside to see if the tents were still there. They were! The morning dew left them a little damp but the oil helped the water to bead up and they were dry in no time. We were the envy of the neighborhood!

Of course we had a designated boy tent and a girl tent. We played in them all morning. Around noon, we made sandwiches and strawberry Kool-Aid and ate our lunches in the tents being oh-so-careful not to spill in our official forts.

The smell of oil was still strong; too strong to sleep in even with the windws propped open.

Finally on about day four we were able to get Mom and Dad's blessings to spend the night in the tents.

This was my first tent outing, so I was really excited!

"So where are you going to pitch them?" Mom asked.

"We thought we would set them up across the drive-through on this side of the crick. That way we won't be too far from home."

The drive-through was the road that looped around the outside perimeter of the trailer court. All the trailers were corralled on the inside of the loop. Just like on the TV show *Wagon Train*. Outside was the woods, crick and tall grass fields.

Before setting up the tents on the sandy hill area near the crick we made sure none of our guests were sleep-walkers (at least an admitted one) because we didn't want them accidentally walking into the fast moving river in the middle of the night or to accidentally wander off in the woods in their sleep.

We grabbed our sleeping bags, pillows, flashlights and s'more supplies and went off to set up camp.

Once we were set up, we combed the area looking for good marshmallow sticks and wood for a campfire. We ate, laughed and told ghost stories until at last we were ready for bed. Dad was a very conscientious camper and instilled his good camping skills in us. Because of this, we had a bucket of water next to the fire to put the flame out before we called it a night. Pour water, stir; pour more water, stir, until we had a pile of muddy wood, ashes and water.

"Good night," we called to one another and settled down for a good night's sleep.

Now, sleeping *in*side and hearing noises, and sleeping *out*side in a tent without your parents or other adult with you are two entirely different things. Inside, in the comfort of your own bed you may think, "Oh, I think I hear a coyote." Outside, without benefit of parents sleeping only a few feet away from you, *any* sound becomes something that will cause a person to freeze in fear, thinking, "WHAT IS THAT???"

No sooner had we fallen asleep when we heard something skittering through our campsite, rustling through dead leaves and twigs.

"What was that?" I whispered to Nita.

"Probably just a mouse," she whispered back. "Nothing to worry about."

Suddenly an owl swooped through the campsite and picked up the little skitter sound. It was so close you could hear the rustle of its wing and tail feathers as it swooped down.

"That was pretty close!" I whispered to Nita. "Whatever it was."

"Yeah, really close!" She whispered back.

We both skootched a little closer to one another for protection.

We just started to drift off when another unknown night noise woke both of us.

"What was that???" I said in full voice this time, hoping to scare it off.

"Will you girls be quiet and go to sleep?" one of the boys called out to us.

"It's getting a little scary. Would one of you like to come and stay in our tent with us?" we called to our tent neighbors.

"I'll go," Gary said in pretend disgust. "It's pretty crowded in here with all of us anyway."

Pretty soon he was over in the "girl tent" and we slept peacefully for the rest of the night. Very early the next morning the sun rose over the trees, already warming the day. It was very noticeable in an orange tent – kind of like sleeping in a sunbeam the way the sides glowed orange.

Suddenly we heard clawing and scraping on the sides of both tents. Something ***really big*** was climbing and ripping at the sides! The tent had a trail of holes where the claws left their mark. We all laid very still, too frightened to move.

"What is that?" called Danny from the other tent.

"I'm not sure. What do we do?" Gary asked.

As the sun rose a little higher in the sky, we saw the outline of two large creatures! One on each tent.

"I think they're snapping turtles!" David yelled.

Now we all knew snappers were nothing to mess with. Their jaws are intensely strong and can sever your finger with one chomp! Even if you cut their heads off, their enormous jaws stay clenched for hours!

"What do we do?" asked Dale.

"Ok," David said. "as soon as the turtles are away from the doors, we run on the count of three."

We could always count on David for a plan.

We all assumed a racing stance so we could bolt across to the trailer.

"Is your turtle clear of the door?" David asked.

"Yeah, he's moving toward the back of the tent."

"Then one… two… three… go!"

We all fell over one another as we bolted from the tents like ants pouring out of a log.

We all screamed, "AHHHHHH!" and ran for our homes.

****

Curiosity finally got the best of us and we all slowly came out of the safety of our homes to see what the big reptiles were up to. We watched the ancient turtles for at least an hour and decided that they were crawling up our tents because we were camping in their sandy egg laying territory. They were "she" turtles!

Snappers rarely come out of the water except to lay their eggs. Being nocturnal, they typically lie on the bottom of a lake or stream, moving around at night to eat. Their diets vary from fish, other turtles, weeds, carrion, bugs, crayfish and small animals.

We carefully walked back across the street and got as close to the nesters as we dared and still be able to watch them from a safe distance. We sat on our haunches in case we needed to make a run for it. I guess we foolishly thought they were going to get up and run after us. We were, after all, in the territory of egg-laying snappers.

They were huge, about twenty-two and twenty-five inches across respectively. The two females had dug holes in the warm, loose sand and were laying their eggs while we watched. They appeared to be oblivious to us as they went about their business.

We watched quietly as the soft, leathery eggs plopped one after another into the sand. We tried to imagine the process the eggs would go through as they lay quietly incubating in their warm, sandy environment, on their way to becoming living, breathing, tiny little turtles. Nature is filled with mysteries.

"Wow, this is amazing," Billy whispered. "I've never seen such a huge turtle. And laying its eggs right in front of us! I wonder how old these turtles are."

David said, "They can live up to forty years so these could be pretty old. Older than us, that's for sure. See all that moss on their backs?"

Billy turned to stare at David for a few seconds and asked, "How do you know all this stuff?"

"I read," David answered.

When they finished depositing their eggs, the turtles carefully covered them with sand using their powerful back legs. As though they hadn't noticed we were there, they slowly turned back toward the river and disappeared.

We had just witnessed a very important part of the cycle of life.

All of us sat quietly for several minutes, contemplating what we had just seen before we went about our day. We were all honored to have witnessed an event that we may never see again in our lifetime.

We had lots of questions for Mom when we told her what we had just seen.

She didn't know a lot about snappers and suggested we look up some information on them the next time we were near an encyclopedia.

As an adult, I love that ***that*** was the standard answer from all of the adults in our lives. As a kid I always wanted to say, ***just give me the answer!*** By looking it up ourselves, we learned the answer to our question and so much more. It has stirred our inquisitive minds to wanting to know the answers to so many of life's important questions.

Later in life my students would ask me, "How do you know so much?" My standard answer is that I never settled for "I don't know." The answer to everything is out there and you should look it up. The internet has all the answers, but an old encyclopedia can give you so much more.

Chapter 26

A Camp in the Woods

Being a boy, and older than Nita and me, had its advantages.

The boys were always allowed to do more daring things than us so we were left home to imagine what they were up to.

The boys were 9, 10, and 12, so they decided it was time to go out into the deep woods across the crick to see what was there.

They took some of the old wood they had salvaged from the boat and the tree house across the river and found a great place to make a NEW shack.

To hear them talk about it, Nita and I thought they had built an amazing rustic cabin with a makeshift latrine for…well, you know. When it was all finished, Dad went with them to see where they had set up camp in case of any possible emergency. He saw that they had found two trees at the edge of a clearing and lashed a long pole between them. From that, they draped a tarp and staked down one side to make a lean-to. The other side was open to the fire pit that they had created from a ring of big rocks. Mosquito netting was draped around the openings to keep the boys from being eaten alive at night. Not exactly a cabin, but it met their needs.

Once Dad inspected the place, he gave it his stamp of approval and said they were okay to spend the night out in the woods. He was proud of their work.

Dad had been a Boy Scout leader since before the boys were born. He taught us a lot about camping, making fires, building lean-to's and chopping wood. He also taught us the importance of treading lightly on the earth so as not to leave a mess. "People should not know you have been there after you leave," he would tell us. Treading lightly also meant that we should not kill anything we weren't going to eat. Because of this (and because meat was very expensive), we ate a lot of "mystery meat." We ate squirrel, rabbit, porcupine (tastes like pine tree), fish, turtles and frog legs to name a few. Mom was always a good sport and cooked whatever they brought home.

The boys finally decided the time was right to try out their new campsite and they traipsed off into the woods together. They packed all their gear including a Boy Scout hatchet for firewood, their sleeping bags, and their trusted Swiss Army Knives. They also had food, s'more fixings and Mom's round, green metal thermos filled with Kool-Aid.

David was in charge of chopping firewood since he was older and stronger.

As I previously mentioned, deep in the woods - alone – after dark, things sound differently than they do outside your back door with your parents at home.

The boys settled in and decided they needed a fire for their hot dogs and marshmallows and to keep any wildlife away.

The younger boys gathered dead logs and branches so David could begin chopping their firewood.

As David chopped, a deep echo came from somewhere in the woods. "Stop!" Gary put his hand out in front of David's arm as though he were about to go through the windshield of a car. "Listen," he whispered. "There's someone else out here. Every time you chop, someone else does too."

The boys listened intently and then David said, "I don't hear anything," and began chopping again. The chopping sound echoed back.

"Listen! There it is again!"

"Gary, it's just an echo." Still, it made the hairs stand up on the back of David's neck at the thought that someone could be in the woods stalking them.

Again, they listened but once again the chopping stopped.

"We'd better quit making so much noise in case someone comes looking for us. No telling who else is out here in the woods," Gary said. "Besides, I think we have enough wood for one night."

The boys started their fire, found some good roasting sticks and ate their feast of hot dogs, buns and

Kool-Aid. They topped it off with as many s'mores as their stomachs could hold.

"This is the life," Danny sighed.

They all leaned back with their heads cradled in their arms and watched the stars overhead; the moon peering through the leaves. The light danced on their faces as a gentle breeze blew the branches of the trees ever so lightly.

"We are so lucky to live up here in the woods and have all these great places to explore," Gary said.

"Yeah, I wonder how many kids actually get to do this," Danny said. The pine scented night air was beginning to cool as the boys began to have thoughts of going to bed.

"Have you ever seen a bear or a moose up close?" David asked.

"No, only from a distance but I know there's plenty of them around here. There is a kid in my class whose dad shot a bear last fall," Danny said. "He said he goes out hunting for bear every year."

"So what do we do if a bear shows up here?" Gary asked with some fear in his voice."

"I don't know. Run?"

"I read an article in our last *Boys Life Magazine* that said you should try and make yourself as large as possible and make lots of noise by banging pots and pans together," Danny said.

"Well, it's worth a try. Might as well be safe," said David.

The boys looked at all their belongings for something they could all use to make noise.

Well, we could pound on the Kool-Aid thermos. It's the only metal thing we have other than some hammers and an ax. "Mom won't be happy if we bring her thermos home all dented and broken," Danny said. "Well, let's at least drink all the rest of the Kool-Aid so we don't waste it. The boys passed the carafe around until it was empty.

They all let out a loud belch and laughed.

"If it keeps us from being eaten by a bear, I don't think she'll care much," Gary said.

They all laughed at that one.

Well, let's all agree to scream really loud and hit whatever is closest to us.

"Okay, I'll hit Gary," Danny laughed.

"Shall we practice?" David asked.

"No, we don't want that other camper out in the woods to come running," Gary said.

"Okay, whisper practice," said Danny.

They all pretended to make as much noise as they could while they whispered, "ahhhhh!" until they were satisfied that they would indeed scare a bear away if it dared come into their camp.

"You know what," said David, "there were lots and lots of ferns around us. If we picked them and put them under our sleeping bags, we would have a soft bed for the night."

They all thought this sounded like a great idea, so they separated and each came back with a pile with which to make their beds.

"I'm tired," said David. Let's get some sleep."

"I have to pee first," said Gary. "I drank way too much Kool-Aid; I don't want to wake up in a wet sleeping bag."

They all decided that was a good idea and stood in a row at the edge of the clearing and relieved themselves.

"You know," Danny said. "There's something special about being able to pee right out in the open air."

"Yeah," said David. "Can you imagine what Martha would say if she saw us doing this?" They all laughed at the thought.

"Royal would laugh," said Danny.

"Yeah," said David, "Royal would love this."

"Well, let's call it a night and go to bed," David said.

"Sure glad you brought the mosquito spray Gary, or we wouldn't have to worry about bears," Danny said. "The mosquitos would eat us alive first!"

The fresh air made the boys very tired, and they all settled down for a good night's sleep.

Sometime in the middle of the night they were awakened by the cry of a large wildcat. It sounded like a lynx or a bobcat! Maybe a mountain lion. He was close but the boys were unable to tell exactly where he was. The terrified young boys huddled together as they stared into the dark woods. The fire had died out and their flashlights would only shine so far. Their eyes burned a hole into the darkness, but they couldn't see beyond the flashlights. They huddled together and thought about looking larger than they were. Did that work for wild cats the way it does for a bear, they wondered?

Their muscles were so tense by now that their bodies ached, but the boys were afraid to move in case the cat moved in from behind them. Their ears strained at any movement beyond the comfort of their flashlights. They decided to sit in a ring with their backs together so they could see from all angles. They were too afraid to cry and shook with fear.

"What do we do?" Gary asked with fear in his voice.

"We've got to light the fire again right now," David said. "Dad said wild cats are afraid of people so start talking and singing really loud and I'll get the fire going.

The boys talked and yelled and sang all the camp songs they could think of at the top of their lungs in order keep the big cat at bay.

At last, the fire was going again and they kept it fed for the rest of the night. They were afraid to take their eyes away from where they heard the cry of the big cat lest the animal creep up and pounce on them from out of the darkness. It frightened them to think that a large, wild cat could be stalking them in the dark from somewhere in the woods. They heard rustling just beyond the light.

The boys knew there were wolves in the woods and they had heard of a wild dog pack attacking cattle on a farm down the road. During the time they lived in the woods they had seen deer, bobcats and even a martin on a nearby trail. The rustling could have been anything.

When the sun was finally beginning to rise above the trees, the boys doused their fire and stirred the charred wood, doused it again and stirred, gathered their belongings and headed for home.

When they were halfway home, David suddenly stopped at the edge of the woods and cried loudly, "Something's wrong, I can't see!"

"What do you mean, you can't see?" Danny asked.

Danny and Gary went over to look at David and gasped!

"David, you should see yourself!" Gary said. "Your whole face looks like a balloon! Your eyes are completely swollen shut!"

"What did you do?" Danny asked.

David started to cry. At least Gary and Danny thought he was crying. They couldn't tell because his eyes were so badly swollen. There were definitely water drops coming from where his eyes should have been so he must have been crying.

"Here, we'll lead you home," Gary said. "I'll just leave my stuff here and come back for it."

David's hands and feet began to swell and he broke out in large red spots that were quickly beginning to swell together into one great big spot.

"Poor David!" Danny exclaimed. "I hope he's not contagious."

Mom gasped when she saw David's face. "Oh my gosh, what happened to you, David?" She was trying not to laugh since he was starting to look like a blimp with arms and legs.

"I can't see," David cried. "My eyes are swollen shut and I itch all over!"

Mom was an LPN (Licensed Practical Nurse) so she knew what to do as soon as she saw him. Mom filled the bathtub with cool water and baking soda and had him soak for several minutes. After his soaking, she gave him an antihistamine to help with the swelling. Lucky for David, Mom worked the night shift so she could keep an eye on him the rest of the day.

"What did you eat?" she asked David. David told her what they had for supper.

"Well that's nothing you haven't eaten before. What else did you guys do out in the woods?" Mom asked.

Danny and Gary looked at each other with questioning eyes.

They told her about all of their adventures throughout the night.

"That still doesn't sound like anything that would cause the swelling," Mom said.

"We slept on some ferns so we wouldn't have to sleep on the ground," Gary said.

"That has to be it! David, you are highly allergic to ferns!" Mom said.

The boys told mom all about someone else in the woods (that one made her smile) and about the bobcat or lynx that they heard.

"Well, you boys had quite a night. Did you get any sleep?"

"Not really," said Danny. "In fact, I think I'm going to go to bed."

"Me too," said David and Gary.

And the three young campers slept well into the afternoon.

Chapter 27

The Bobcat

The boy's bobcat/lynx/mountain lion camping story ran rampant through the Cohasset School. With each telling, the story became more and more legendary and so did the boys who experienced it. Tales of their bravery spread like wildfire and their story even made it to the Grand Rapids newspaper!

This was big stuff for three young boys in a very small town.

A few days later Marvin knocked on our door looking very pale.

"Marvin, what's wrong?" Danny asked.

"I was having a hard time sleeping last night because I swear I heard the bobcat – or whatever it was - right outside my bedroom window. I was so scared I couldn't sleep the rest of the night. I mean, what if it came in through my bedroom window or something?"

"Maybe we should go looking for it," Danny suggested.

"I don't know. It could be really dangerous. I know they're shy, but what if it has babies nearby or something. It could get awfully mean! We could be putting our lives on the line."

We saw Dale walking over from the trailer next door.

"Hey, did you guys hear that something got into Billy's chicken coop and killed a bunch of his chickens? He said there are feathers everywhere."

With that we all looked at one another. "Bobcat!" We all said simultaneously.

"Ok, now we have to do something," Marvin said. "If you won't help me, I'll go it alone."

"Marv, you can't do that! It's too dangerous! It could even be rabid. We need to come up with a plan that involves all of us," David said.

Just then we heard Nita scream and come running across the road in tears. She was hysterical! "Something killed my rabbit during the night! Oh, poor Whitey!"

(I often wondered what people would name their pets if they didn't have a color.)

"Alright, we can't let this go on any longer," Gary said. "We need to take action today!"

We decided to scour the woods that surrounded the trailer court and look for evidence of the big cat.

"Look very carefully because they blend into the forest so well. We could be looking right at it and not see it," David warned.

So we went to the woods, split up into small groups and began our search. We proudly thought of ourselves as early Native Americans we were so stealthy. Not a sound; not so much as a twig snap as we scoured the forest. We were good but there was no sign of the big cat anywhere.

We were heading back to the trailer court when we heard Marv's mom call out. "Here it is! It's in the garage!"

We ran as fast as we could and met up with his excited mom.

"I was about to back the car out when I saw the bobcat staring at me from the rafters. I ran out of the garage and closed the door. I know it's still in there."

Bobcats are the smallest and most common of the three wild cats in northern Minnesota. They're about twice as tall as a housecat and can be up to four feet in length including their bobbed tail, depending on whether it's male or female. Bobcats in the northern forested areas tend to be larger and darker in color than those living further south. At one time their range extended into southern Minnesota but are now found primarily in the northern part of the state. They are fierce predators and can take down an animal up to eight times its weight. Singularly they are able take down a deer or large domestic animal such as a sheep or young cow.

We armed ourselves with baseball bats and rakes and went into the garage. Nobody had any idea about how to get the bobcat out of the rafters let alone what this animal was capable of doing to us.

There was a small ten-inch opening in the side of the garage, so the boys told me to stand there with a baseball bat and hit the cat over his head when he came out.

Now, I wasn't crazy about the idea of killing an animal, so my heart wasn't really into my job. Like the obedient little sister that I was though, I stood next to the hole with the baseball bat high above my head – waiting for my big moment. I could hear the kids running around, clunking and shouting in the garage and an occasional yowl from the bobcat but so far there was no action from where I was standing. I was beginning to feel like a right fielder at a baseball game and my mind began to wander. The bat was getting really heavy, so I rested it on my shoulder. I had to keep reminding myself to pay attention. I thought about putting my eye up to the hole to see how the kids were doing at getting the cat out of the garage but decided that was possibly a bad idea.

So, I waited…

Suddenly a streak of brown fur flew through the hole. It ran so fast I couldn't even identify it as a bobcat. I did manage to bring the bat down seconds after I saw the streak, but there was no way I was going to hit it. I still wonder how it ever got through such a small opening without skinning itself.

Dan came around the corner of the garage expecting to see a pile of fur under my bat. "Elaine! Why didn't you hit him? That was your job!!!"

"Come on! I'm six, did you really think I was going to hit something I didn't even know was coming?"

Danny stomped off completely disgusted at his incompetent little sister.

We never heard from the bobcat again although that doesn't mean it wasn't watching us from afar.

Chapter 28

The Fishing Expedition

Up north, it's not uncommon to see several people fishing off bridges at any given time. The power lines that hover over the top of the bridges are adorned with an odd assortment of fishing line and tackle that found its way around the wires during robust casts into the water. It's important to bring a good supply of tackle if you fish from the bridge.

***

Now that Dad had given the boys permission to use the boat, they put it to good use as often as they were allowed. No more fishing over the side of the bridge for them! They packed up their usual sandwiches and the metal thermos of lime Kool-Aid and set out to fish in the Mississippi. With a real boat the boys felt the entire Mississippi river was theirs. Sometimes they rowed as far as two miles up the river and always returned with a stringer of fish. Every fishing trip was a new adventure for the three young boys. They took turns rowing because it was quite a long distance for their young muscles to row from our place on the Bass River into the Mississippi. They had set out early in the morning, so they had plenty of time to fish, eat lunch, and get back home.

"I know," suggested Danny. "How about if we say whoever isn't rowing gets to troll behind the boat. We're sure to catch some extra fish that way."

"Okay, good idea," David agreed.

They all baited their hooks and were ready to fish. When they were about a mile upstream, they threw their lines in trolled, and took turns rowing. They had been keeping an eye on the sky and noticed black clouds were quickly rolling in. Suddenly it began to rain. Hard! The rain soon became a fierce downpour and the boys could barely see one other in the same boat. They rowed with all their might while one bailed water over the side of the boat. They had decided they needed to turn back and go downriver to the safety of the bridge. When they reached the bridge, they tied the boat off on one of the pilings and watched the curtain of rain close them off from the rest of the world. Thank goodness it wasn't lightning, or they would have been in serious trouble being under a steel bridge. In a metal boat. On the water.

As they sat watching the rain pour around them, there was nothing else to do but fish, so they dropped their lines over the side of the boat. Within seconds first one boy and then another pulled a flopping crappie into the boat. *Huge* crappies, the size of a dinner plate! One measured a foot long according to the embossed ruler on the top of David's tackle box. By the time the rain stopped they had a stringer full of the largest crappies they had ever seen! The feast that evening was both sumptuous and unforgettable.

On future fishing trips the boys tied up to the pilings many times but never again caught even a *little* crappie in the same spot. Apparently, the fish had joined the boys in taking the same refuge under the bridge on that rainy day. To a hungry family, they were a gift from heaven.

The Mississippi took care of a poor family in rough times. It was a mentor that taught all of us (mostly the boys) self-reliance and delight in simple pleasures. It was a dear friend to us for many years to come.

Chapter 29

Skunk Trouble

Dad always taught the boys that you clean what you catch. He taught us how to clean and filet the fish. The rest was up to us.

After catching an abundance of fish earlier in the day, it was time to get them cleaned. David and Gary were off taking care of the boat, tackle and rods so Dan set out to clean their catch.

Our neighborhood was beset with a good share of feral cats. Sadly, people would move away and leave their cats behind to fend for themselves. Being good hunters by nature, it was assumed they would be fine on their own. Unfortunately, other wildlife and brutal winters often made their chances of survival slim.

Each of the boys had claimed a cat for themselves and we all enjoyed their company. Dad was not particularly fond of cats, so they were not allowed to stay in the already overcrowded trailer. During the bitterly cold northern Minnesota winters, we allowed them to stay in the enclosed, but unheated porch with spare blankets so they wouldn't freeze to death.

Danny's cat was a particularly friendly, beautiful black and white tuxedo cat that liked to follow him at every opportunity.

As Dan stood at the cleaning table scaling, gutting and fileting the fish that the boys had caught, the cat jumped up next to him to see what his owner was up to. "No, you don't," Danny said as he gently set the cat down on the ground. "This is *our* supper and we don't need cat fur on all of this good meat." The cat sat behind him contentedly eating the fish remains being tossed to him.

Soon other cats came to enjoy the fruits of the boys' labors while Danny, deftly scaled, cut and tossed the innards and heads to them.

He finished with his job and had the filets all neatly piled in a basin; but as he turned to go up to the trailer, he suddenly froze in his tracks.

As the cats wandered away with their bellies full of fresh fish, a skunk had walked up and taken their place. Danny had didn't quite know what to do. If he ran, he would likely startle the skunk and get sprayed. He was literally scared stiff as the skunk was only a couple of feet behind him merrily munching on his free repast.

It was obvious that the skunk wasn't rabid, or he would have bitten Danny by now.

Danny thought carefully about what to do.

Finally, he decided the skunk was happy! He wasn't going to spray anybody as long as he was getting food, so Danny just decided to keep tossing fish pieces to the skunk until he contentedly walked away with a full belly.

And that's just what he did.

Danny let out a sigh of relief as he watched the fluffy black and white tail disappear back into the woods.

Chapter 30

Leaving

Dad came home one evening, sat us all down and revealed the sad news that he had taken a job down in the Twin Cities. We would be moving in two weeks.

Mom knew this was coming, of course; but we kids had no idea that this was going to happen.

The five of us sat with our mouths open in shocked disbelief. Never *ever* did we think we would have to move.

Maybe we were hearing this wrong. Maybe we were all having the same bad dream.

Our eyes were beginning to well with tears as we listened to Dad explain why we had to leave. He said the jobs in the mines were drying up and he needed to find work to support us. He had just accepted a job with the electrical union, and he needed to report to work in two weeks. He sympathized with us and realized how difficult this was on all of us. My dad grew up in Hibbing, so his roots were deeply seated in the North Country as well. Mom had come down from Canada so she too loved life in the woods.

"We're not moving out of state kids. We can come by and see your friends whenever we go up to see Martha and Royal and your grandparents. Your mom and I don't want to leave either, but we really have no choice. We need money to live."

Mom said her brother was going to come down from Zim with his farm truck to take our trailer down to Shakopee (shock'- uh-pee) where we would live until our new house would be built.

We didn't own much so there wasn't much to pack up. We put breakables in boxes to be driven down to the Cities in the station wagon or piled in the boat which we towed behind us. The rest was tied down and secured in the trailer in hopes that it wouldn't fall out of their designated areas.

We walked throughout the trailer court and the rest of the town and said our sad goodbyes to the friends that had truly become more like brothers and sisters to us. They were our comrades, our classmates and our fellow adventurers during the time that we had been with them.

Mom notified the school that we would be leaving and got our records to take with us to our new school.

Mom's brother Hillary arrived early Saturday morning and He and Dad got the trailer ready to roll. After they unhooked the plumbing and propane lines from the trailer, Hillary slowly pulled forward and began moving the trailer from our lot. As the trailer pulled forward and away from our lot, we noticed the ragged looking pile of wood that had served us well through so many projects and big dreams. Hopefully it would ignite someone else's imagination and become yet another project.

The empty lot where our trailer stood just moments ago, left a large gap-toothed hole in the middle of the court. Much like the holes that were now in our hearts.

Faces were long and the tears flowed freely as we got into the car and made a final loop around the court, waving a sad good-bye to friends and acquaintances.

Part of me didn't want to look as we pulled out, but the other part wanted to take everything in so I would never forget this wonderful place. We drove down the dirt road to the main highway out of town that would eventually lead to our new home.

I don't think any of us said a word all the way to Shakopee.

Our hearts would forever remain behind in the North Country. As we drove the long journey to our new home, nobody asked if we were there yet or picked on each other to pass the time. We just watched out the window without a word as the landscape changed from thick pine woods, lake and bogs to larger towns and deciduous trees.

I can imagine that our friends back at the trailer court felt terribly lost without the Brunet family there. We were the "idea kids." Nobody ever had to think about what they should do next because all they had to do was to come to our neighborhood and see what the Brunets were up to. Being bored was never part of our vocabulary. We had David so we always had someone with a plan.

Over the months that followed we learned that several other mining employees found other work as well, and one by one they moved away but some of them were lucky enough to stay somewhere up north.

***

Eventually we would live in a real house, but we had to wait for our new house to be built.

In the meantime, we found a trailer court within 30 miles from where our house was being built. We could set the trailer there until it would be time to move again.

The trailer court was just off the main highway coming into town and had a lovely, fast flowing, shallow stream that meandered next to the area. Of course, that would eventually mean adventure to us.

We enrolled in school for the second time in the year.

The school didn't provide free bus service. What it would have cost our parents for us to ride the bus to and from school was way beyond what they could afford. Dad needed to leave early with the car to get to work on time, so our only choice was to walk the mile to and from school.

Soon it was January.

All people who live in the northern states know January is without a doubt the worst month of the year. It was bitterly cold, and the wind howled on an almost daily basis. There were no trees sheltering the trailers, so we felt the wind much more than we did in

Cohasset. Everything seemed to shake. January is the month you just do your best to survive until you make it to February and March and finally the promise of spring.

Every morning with Mom's help, we bundled ourselves up until we could barely move through all the sweaters, tights, long johns, extra pants, coats, hats, double mittens, choppers and scarves. Heaven forbid someone would forget to use the bathroom before they were all dressed, or they had to start all *over* again. Those who were ready to go went outside to wait so they didn't melt under all the clothes while they waited for the ne'er-do-well who wasn't planning ahead. Our mantra became *don't forget to use the bathroom before you get all your clothes on!*

The school reminded us of our old school in Cohasset although quite a bit larger and surrounded by houses. It seemed odd to be somewhere that was strangely familiar but with all new faces. We made new friends but tried not to get too attached to them, knowing that our stay would only be temporary. We would be moving again in the spring.

We eventually got used to the long walk to and from school although I always lagged behind due to the bundles of clothing we had to wear to stay warm. I was in first grade at the time so the boys would get tired of having to slow down until I caught up with them. Nita was just a little older than I was, so she was good about staying with me while the boys scampered off.

***

One afternoon as we were walking home from school, the wind picked up something fierce and it made my eyes water so that I could barely see. My eyelashes stuck together, and tears were frozen to my face. The temperature for the day was already well below zero and the added wind chill made it feel about 40 below. My scarf and hat were caked with frost from being over my mouth and eyes. I was lagging well beyond the rest of the group when a big, fancy black car pulled up next to me. The man rolled his window down to talk to me. "Oh, honey, you look so cold!"

"I'm freezing!" I hollered back as I stood there shivering. How dare he say something so stupid to a child when he was sitting in his warm, comfortable car.

"Why don't you get in the car and I'll give you a ride home?"

He had well oiled black hair and I thought he looked a bit like a slightly thinner version of Jackie Gleason. He smelled of cheap men's cologne, booze and cigarettes. His voice was smooth and inviting, but most of all, the car was warm and enticing since he had turned the heat up as high as it would go prior to rolling down his window. This guy was good.

"I'm not supposed to get in the car with strangers," I said.

"It's ok," he smiled. "I know your father."

"You do?" I asked hopefully. "What's his name?"

"Well… I know him very well. Let's see, his name is…um…what *is* his name? Gosh, I can't think of it right now, but I know you live down this road."

"Paul."

His face suddenly lit up. "That's it, his name is Paul! See, I told you I know who he is. Now, why don't you get in and I'll take you home?" He leaned across the car and opened the passenger side door. The warmth from the car's heater was enticing.

"Can you take my brothers and sister?" I pointed in their direction and said, "They're right there and they're cold too."

He looked at the other kids and I saw the expression on his face cloud a bit as he anticipated this new problem.

His voice cheered up again as he turned and spoke to me. "Well, I don't think I have enough room for that many kids. I'll be glad to take *you* home though."

"Well, let me tell them that I have a ride home, okay?"

"If you just get in the car we can drive up to where your brothers and sister are, and you can tell them."

Suddenly out of nowhere, Nita came running up from behind me. She grabbed my arm and ran, knocking me off my feet, pulling me behind. "We're walking!" she yelled angrily at the man as she kept running down the sidewalk trailing me behind her.

When we were well away from the car, we watched the man speed away.

"Nita, that was rude! Remember, Dad said we should be nice to everyone," I yelled.

Nita pulled my arm hard and spun me around to face her.

"Don't you EVER get into a stranger's car! That's so dangerous!"

The boys came walking back to see what we were yelling about.

"Elaine almost got into a car with a stranger!" Nita said.

"He said he knew Dad! He knew his name!" I whined.

"How could he have known Dad's name?" Gary asked. "We just moved here; we don't know anybody yet."

"Well…he couldn't remember Dad's name at first, so I told him what it was," I said.

"How could you be so stupid?" Danny yelled. "Everyone knows you don't get in the car with a stranger!"

"Come on guys," David said. "We need to be better about staying with her while we're walking; she's just a little kid. We need to slow down and keep an eye on her."

We walked home the last half mile without saying a word. We quietly glanced at one another, wondering what our parents were going to say when we got home. Should we even tell them? Life could have suddenly been quite different had I gotten in the car with the man just a few minutes earlier. We were all suddenly more aware of how dangerous life could be and how we needed to be more careful with one another.

    I often worry whether he stopped yet another little girl further down the road.

    I pray he didn't.

Chapter 31

The Final Move

With our new house complete, we loaded up the trailer once again, hauled it up to Cedar Grove and backed it into the driveway of our new home. It looked so small next to our new three-bedroom rambler! While standing out in the driveway comparing the house and the trailer, Nita and I commented that it was hard to believe that all seven of us fit into that tiny trailer.

Although we tried not to complain, our new housing location was fairly awful! It wasn't a town; it was just the beginnings of a housing project in the middle of farm country. We were the thirteenth house in what would eventually be a large housing project of modest, middle-class homes.

We all enrolled in our third and final school for the year. We went to Burnsville school which was K-12 at the time.

It began to rain.

And rain.

The mud around our housing area was a foot deep on future roads and the yards were worse. It reeked of cow manure to the point that we were unable to open the windows to let cool air in. There were 2 x 10 boards everywhere so we could get around without sinking.

The mud often kept us from getting to school, as the busses were unable to make their way to our street without getting stuck. We often lost our shoes and socks trying to run the two long blocks through the gooey mud in hopes of catching the bus (my favorite black, patent leather shoes are permanently sealed under the pavement somewhere on County Road 30 – now Diffley Road).

There were large, deep holes dug every so many feet in preparation for future basements that would also have future houses and lawns that would eventually contain grass, flowers and sapling trees. We just had to wait for the future to decide if we were going to like it here.

Right now, the verdict was definitely out since we had to stay in the house due to the mud. Besides, there were no kids our age in the neighborhood. We were being held captive by mud! We weren't used to watching TV but that's what we had, so that's what we did.

As the long, cold winter finally had given way to spring and then summer, we found that the future basements in our area and the huge amounts of rain and melted snow made great swimming holes, and we took advantage of them as often as we could.

During our swimming expeditions, we kept having our legs brushed by something that must have been fish. It was a little unnerving since we spent a lot of time watching sci-fi movies. What could be lurking beneath the surface? Will it drag us to the bottom of the hole before someone can save us?

One finally did come close enough to see it and we picked it up.

"What in the world is this?" Danny asked. It wasn't a fish, or a salamander. So, what was it?

We decided to show Mom.

We ran home with the funny looking little guy, found a jar and put it in some water.

"Oh, it's a mudpuppy! We used to catch these all the time when we were kids," Mom said.

We had no idea what a mudpuppy was, so we went to the encyclopedia to find out more about them.

They are interesting, but funny looking little creatures with beady wide-set eyes and an ever present wide, grin. They reminded us of the many bullheads we used to catch in the crick.

They usually live under logs and rocks in rivers, streams and lakes. Mudpuppies are nocturnal and never leave the water, even though they have legs.. At night, they feed on whatever meat they can find (crayfish, worms, snails, etc.). If the water is too murky, they will come out of hiding during the day. Apparently, we were stirring up way too much mud for their liking because they were everywhere as soon as we jumped into the water! They measured about six to eight inches long and have frilly gills that make them look like they're all dressed up to go out. The encyclopedia said they could get up to 13 inches long, but we never saw anything that large. These funny little creatures are sometimes called water dogs and make squeaky vocalizations that resemble the bark of a puppy. These gentle little creatures provided us with hours of entertainment once we finally determined we weren't being attacked by some underwater horror movie…thing.

Houses were built quickly, covering the basement swimming holes. Families with kids began moving into the area. An elementary school was eventually built within two blocks from us.

The boys made several close lifelong friends, much like back in the trailer court. They remain in touch even to this day. Nita and I were still best friends, but eventually there were other kids in the neighborhood that we found to play with as well.

There was a large round pond across the street between us and the school that was probably for cattle back when the area was someone's pasture. Now, however, it was a retention pond for street runoff and it quickly became our main source of entertainment. The newly paved roads and sewer systems allowed the pond to fill quickly so we had a good-sized play area and there were plans to make a park around the pond. The pond was surrounded by a wide, sloping hill that was perfect for sledding in the winter months. There were a handful of large scrub oak trees that provided climbing and, of course, tree forts.

Things were slowly looking up!

Chapter 32

A Close Call

August brought extreme heat and humidity to the Cities. It had already been a miserably hot summer!

We thanked God for the luxury of the pond where we could head across the street and go swimming any time we wanted.

We kids had put a lot of work into cleaning the area up so we wouldn't be tripping over dead trees or garbage under the water. We were pretty proud of our work as the resident pond patrol.

Two of the kids who lived across the street from the pond had become our constant companions. They loved to see what the Brunet kids were up to since we knew how to have a good time.

"Let's go swimming. It's too hot to do anything else," Nita said.

We grabbed all the flotation devices we could find and headed for the pond.

My friend Cheryl and I were sitting on an air mattress while Nita was in an inner tube pushing us around. Everyone else had their own floatee of some sort and we were slowly floating and enjoying the day. I mention that we were *sitting* on the air mattress – bad idea. It wasn't a heavy-duty mattress that you would sleep on; it was just a cheap flimsy model, meant to last a week or less.

One of the two of us moved ever so slightly and both of us toppled into the water in opposite directions. Nita grabbed Cheryl and pulled her onto the inner tube, but I went straight to the bottom of the pond.

At first the kids thought I was kidding, and they waited for me to come back up to the surface; but I didn't.

I have never been a strong swimmer and was even less so back then.

In Minnesota there were public safety announcements on television during the summer months warning people not to cry for help unless they really needed it. If you *did* need help, you should yell *HELP!* as loud as you can. That was all I could think of. Yell "help" so people would know I was drowning.

After several seconds, I made it to the surface, took a large gasp of air and whispered HELP as loud as I could. That's all that I could get out just a whisper.

I instantly went straight to the bottom again as though someone was pulling me back under the water.

By this time the kids realized that I was in trouble.

Danny was the strongest swimmer of the group, so he went down to find me and pull me to the surface.

And that was when things became very strange.

My outside body was thrashing like crazy and I could see legs kicking over my head, so I knew the situation from up above me was pretty frantic. Poor Danny tried as hard as he could to grab me so he could pull me to safety, but I fought him with every ounce of my being.

From my *inside* body, things were very different. I suddenly became two different people in the same body. My mind was completely relaxed, and I was thoroughly enjoying what was happening around me. The sun, dancing on the water droplets suddenly became crystal clear jewels swirling all around me. I was mesmerized by their beauty as they swirled over and around my head as though they were little fairies dancing for my amusement. I couldn't take my eyes off them and they made me smile!

The water in the murky pond became clear as glass in a large ring around me and I suddenly had the inexplicable feeling that the water had become the cleanest, freshest air I could ever breathe Something was encouraging me to take a big deep breath and fill my lungs with it.

I surfaced again, tried to yell "help" and was down again. It was just a cursory yell because at this point, I really didn't care if anyone saved me or not. I was enjoying my surroundings beneath the water and would have been okay staying right where I was.

Danny continued his frantic quest to try and grab me, but my body was fighting him for all I was worth.

I felt sorry for the kids above me because I knew they were all scared and beginning to panic. I wanted to tell them that I was fine and how beautiful the water below the surface was, but I couldn't.

In desperation, Danny took another big breath, dove back down, grabbed me by the hair and finally got me to shore. Once I reached shore I continued to try and yell for help. I whispered over and over until my voice was finally working.

"You stupid idiot!" Danny yelled and pushed me out of the way. "Why did you fight me when I was trying to save you?" He stomped away and went home. I could tell that what had just happened clearly scared him far more than it did me.

It's difficult to explain, but I was truly changed after that day. Many who have experienced the same situation would later describe it as a near death experience. I never thought of death as scary or sad from that day on.

Chapter 33

The Perfect Birthday Present

"You know, Mom's birthday is coming up next month. We should get her something really great this year," Gary said.

"Yeah, she's awfully good to us. I wonder what she would like," David replied.

Danny was sitting with the latest *Outdoor Life* magazine. "Hey, I know!" he said. "Look at this ad. We can get her a monkey! You know how she loves animals; a monkey would be perfect for her!"

We all gathered around Danny to read the ad.

"See?" he said. We can get this cute little squirrel monkey for $29.99 plus shipping and handling. How much money does everyone have?"

Collectively we came up with $30.00 so we still needed to raise the money for shipping and handling.

"Have you guys all collected from your customers for the month?" David asked.

The boys all had paper routes and back then you had to go door-to-door to collect what the customers owed for their newspaper.

They decided that they had collected all the money they were owed, so we needed to think of another way to make up the difference.

"How about Dad?" Gary asked. "I'll bet he would like to go in on this present."

"Hmmm. Dad's not the animal lover that Mom is. I don't know how he'll feel about a monkey.

"We really need to let him know about our idea before he discovers we have a monkey in the house. What about if we offer to work for the money?" Nita asked.

"Well, all we can do is ask," I said.

That evening we pulled Dad into the bedroom so we could reveal our plan. He laughed skeptically. "Are you sure this is such a good idea?" he asked. "I think I need to think about this for a while. Let me give you an answer tomorrow. By the way, do you even know what monkeys eat?"

"Ooo, good question," Gary said.

That sent us in search of the encyclopedia to find out what to feed our monkey (Mom's monkey). We called pet stores to see if they sold monkey food and even called the zoo for advice. Their advice was not to get a monkey because they should be left in the wild. We should have listened to them..

The next day, as promised, Dad gathered us together in a secret location and said we could go ahead and order the monkey. He would build a large cage for and keep it hidden from Mom until after the monkey arrived. I'm not sure what he had in mind for hiding a six by four by six-foot cage, but I figured he must have had an plan.

We all ran outside every time the delivery truck went through the neighborhood, hoping that they were going to drop off the best birthday present a bunch of kids ever gave to their mother.

At last it finally arrived, just in time for Mom's birthday!

We wrapped the small crate in newspaper and put a bow on it. The five of us brought it to Mom with smiles so broad our faces must have looked as though they were about to crack. We hoped she wouldn't notice that the box was beginning to smell.

Somehow, I have a feeling Dad must have warned Mom what was about to happen. Just in case. How else would he explain a six-foot cage in the basement?

Mom was laughing so hard just looking at our faces; it was all she could do to open her miracle gift.

The box neglected to add a disclaimer that the poor monkey had been taken *directly* out of the jungle, shoved inside a small crate, stuck on a plane, and woe to the first person to open the crate.

At last Mom was about to open the crate and we all sat holding our breath expecting the adorable little creature to gingerly crawl out of his container, give us all a big hug and be our new forever friend. Just like Cheetah on the Tarzan movies we watched on TV every Saturday night.

No sooner had Mom opened her gift when a wild streak of brown fur and tail flew out of the crate, landed on Mom's arm and bit down hard in several places drawing blood with every bite! From there, it ran around the house going from room to room, screaming at the top of its lungs and finally landed on the top of the drapes.

We ran after him in hopes of containing the little guy.

"Don't chase him," Mom warned. "He's terrified He needs to get used to us. Just let him land somewhere."

The poor little guy sat up there for a very long time, leaving a long trail of poop running down Mom's drapes.

Mom was sure she would be able to pick him up, but when she tried, the monkey (whom she named Tiny – another very thoughtful name) bared his teeth and lunged, daring her to try and pick him up. She laughed at her new birthday gift as Tiny threatened to bite her fingers off. She thanked us for her new little creature, and I think she was genuinely pleased. Mom is a very unique individual – always up for a new adventure and always a good sport.

She went to the kitchen and got a piece of banana and some water and offered it to her new little friend. He took it from her fingers (without biting them) and ate and drank with wild abandon. Who knows when he last had anything to eat or drink? Thank goodness there are now regulations against taking wild creatures out of their habitats and legally putting them on the market like someone did to this poor scared little creature.

Mom coaxed her frightened little monkey off the curtain rod and attached a leash to the collar that the little guy had around his waist. She carefully took him downstairs and put him in his big new cage with a helping of more fruits and some pellets that came with Tiny. We left him to sleep and relax for the night.

Life with a monkey was interesting to say the least.

During the years that Tiny lived with us, we were never really able to tame him, but then he had been born wild.

He seemed to know that Mom was his person as she was the only one who was easily able to pick him up and snuggle with him. He had good taste in people.

Squirrel monkeys have a unique method of protecting themselves by defecating (pooping) down the back of the person whose shoulder he's riding on. They also "claim you" by peeing in their hands and wiping the urine all over you. This kind of "love" is not always welcomed by the owners.

While taking him on bike rides, we tried to avoid groups of children who would run up to us exclaiming, *Oh look! It's a monkey* because we knew it meant having to go home to change clothes. One would think the barred teeth and lunging would tell kids to stay away because he WILL bite, but they insisted that the monkey would love to have all the attention they could dish out.*

Tiny adapted quite well to his urban jungle. He discovered that he could run from house to house throughout the neighborhood by crossing the telephone wires. We never worried about him because he always came back and everyone knew whom he belonged to. His house to house ventures became longer and longer until one time he didn't come home for several days.

"Don't worry, he knows where he lives and will come home when he's hungry," Mom said.

Mom was always right about everything so as usual, we trusted her and didn't worry. Much.

My parents were in the process of having a fireplace installed in the basement. The brick mason showed up early one morning to work on our new structure and headed downstairs as usual.

We were all in the kitchen eating breakfast when we heard a bloodcurdling scream from downstairs.

"Tiny's home," Gary said grinning, as though the doorbell had just rung.

We all smiled and returned to our breakfasts.

The mason came up the stairs looking as white as a ghost and gasped, "There's a monkey in your basement!"

"Oh, ok, thanks for letting us know," Danny said.

"No, you don't understand. (The poor man was shaking terribly.) A *live* monkey dropped down through the chimney and landed on my head while I was working on the fireplace. He just dropped down out of nowhere. He ran back up the chimney when I screamed."

"Yup, that would be our monkey. He's been staying out at night so I'm glad to know he came home. Thanks for telling us," I said.

"You're welcome, but could you please put him in his cage? I'm not sure I like him sitting on my head while I'm working. He keeps barring his teeth and batting at me."

"Okay. I'm sorry he scared you," David said and went down to take care of Tiny.

Had we been older, we would have realized that the poor man could have had a heart attack and died of fright when Tiny dropped on his head. I'm glad He was okay.

***

Frustrated that we were never able to thoroughly enjoy Tiny's company without a clothing change or some nasty bites, Mom decided it was time to give her little friend up. She put an ad in the Minneapolis newspaper, and lo and behold an elderly lady called! She had been looking for a male squirrel monkey as she had a little female! She took Tiny home with her and I assume he was able to live happily ever after with his new companion.

It all ended well.

Chapter 34

Spear Fishing

We lived a couple of miles from the Minnesota River. For the boys, it was just a bike ride away.

As soon as they were home from school, they gathered their spears or guns on an almost daily basis to hunt ducks or go spear fishing, depending on the season.

On this particular day, spear fishing was on their mind. In the past few weeks, they had been hunting carp, buffalo head and eelpout.

Their favorite fishing and hunting spot was just off the Cedar Avenue bridge which crosses the Minnesota river.

Now, David was smart, but he was also very clumsy and prone to injuring himself.

Along the side of the bridge was a pipe that they walked on to get to their fishing area. It was almost level with the road and was slippery with moss and water.

Fifteen feet below, the water was shallow and curved like an oxbow. There was enough water for the fish to go back and forth while the boys waited for them to swim by.

The street department used to throw large chunks of used cement and rusted pipes in the water so there were lots of very sharp, rusty objects that the boys needed to be careful of.

As they walked along the pipe, with their four-pronged spears in hand, they were being careful not to fall off the pipe onto any of the dangerous objects below.

Suddenly Gary said, "Oh no! David just fell off the pipe!"

"Oh my gosh," Danny said. "I think he might be dead!"

David was lying face down in the muck. Not moving.

"David are you alright?" shouted Gary.

David lifted his head out of the mud and said, "Yeah, I'm fine."

As the two boys looked at him lying on his stomach in the mud, Danny yelled, "David, where is your spear?" Danny feared David might have speared himself in the fall the pain hadn't set in for him to realize that he was seriously wounded.

He felt around and said, "It's right here at my side. I'm okay, really."

When the boys looked at the strange position David was lying in, saw that he miraculously missed landing on every single sharp piece of cement and discarded metal. In fact, it appeared that the junk surrounding him perfectly outlined his body in the position he was laying!

David's guardian angel was working overtime that day.

Chapter 35

The Fly Catcher

By the time I was in fourth grade, we were all finally settling into our new surroundings.

School had begun once again. Gary and Danny were now in junior. high and David was in high school.

I always enjoyed school, but the weather was still hot, so it was hard to concentrate. Without air conditioning in the schools the afternoons could be torture. With a full stomach from lunch, recess in the warm sun, and the teacher reading to us after we settled back in the classroom, I found myself fighting hard to stay awake.

I sat at my desk with my head propped on my hand listening to the story the teacher was reading when my attention became focused on a fly that had settled on my desk. I watched the little insect as he walked across my desk, stopped, cleaned his wings, rubbed his eyes with his front legs, and then continued his furtive venture across my desk. I became fixated with his behavior and totally lost track of the story the teacher was reading, which really bothered me because up until now I was completely enjoying the story.

The fly crouched and then deftly leaped from my desk and landed on my face. I waved him away but secretly hoped he would come back to play on my desk because I was finding him fascinating. No sooner did I have that thought when the fly came back to my desk once again. I continued to watch him as I slowly moved my right hand under my desk and over to the right side until it laid parallel to the fly. Suddenly my hand flew across my desk, and I snatched at the fly!

To my amazement, I realized that I had actually caught him! He was in my hand buzzing at me!

Now what? I let him go, and he didn't bother me the rest of the afternoon. When I did see him flying about the classroom and landing on other kids' desks, I just grinned proudly. I had caught that fly with my own hand.

I didn't know much about flies so, as I was always encouraged to do, I grabbed the encyclopedia when I got home to find out more about the common housefly.

What I learned really grossed me out, and I had a different feeling about the fly that had been trapped in my hand hours earlier. I immediately went to the bathroom and washed my hands.

They carry up to 65 diseases known to humans such as typhoid fever, anthrax and a bunch of other diseases I had never heard of.

House flies don't bite so they can only eat liquid food. They do this by spitting their saliva on whatever they want to eat so it turns to liquid and then they suck it up with their tongues. Ewww! No wonder adults have such a fit when flies land on our picnic food! They drink a lot of water since they are continually regurgitating saliva on food and then pooping it out in little things known as fly specks.

It gets worse.

Although they like sweet things and other foods that are in your house, they really like to eat dead things (animals, fish, trash) and animal feces (especially horse manure). They lay about 100 to 150 eggs in whatever disgusting thing they are feeding on and *then* the eggs hatch and become white worms called maggots!

Houseflies live about two and a half weeks but can survive up to three months if they can find a protected location.

Okay, that did it! Something had to be done with all the flies in our classroom, so I decided to become THE FLYMINATOR!!

As the fall weather began to cool down, flies were looking for every opportunity to come indoors where it's warm. Our classroom quickly filled with the pesky creatures as students went in and out from recess. I wasn't attached to these flies like I was with my first catch. Now that I knew more about them, these flies were gross and annoying. I caught them one after another, shook them up to make them dizzy and quickly threw them hard to the ground to end their miserable lives.

By now the kids around me realized my prowess as a mighty catcher of flies and looked on me with admiration with each catch.

I became obsessed with catching flies and began losing my focus as a student. I was so good I began snatching them out of mid-air as they flew past me. I couldn't miss. My reflexes amazed even me! My eyes scanned the room all day looking for my next victim.

Kids in the class quietly kept score for me and silently cheered me on as I snatched one fly after the next all day long.

The class whiner decided the teacher needed to know what I was doing, and her hand shot high into the air. She glanced at me from the corner of her eye. "Mrs. Friendshoe?" She said as her hand quickly fluttered back and forth to get the teacher's attention. "Mrs. Friendshoe?"

The kids sitting near her shot angry glances in her direction and slowly shook their heads to quell the tattling. "Whiner girl" slowly lowered her hand as she noticed the disapproving looks of those around her. They wanted to see me continue my outstanding fly catching abilities.

What surprised me is that the teacher never caught on to what I was doing. How could she not know?

I could no longer stop my hunting. My obsession worsened by the day. I silently slipped from my desk, crawled across the floor and snuck up on the flies on the other side of the room, went in for the kill, and just as silently crawled across the floor and slid back into my desk. Nobody looked in my direction; they just smiled slyly at my prowess and continued working. The kids never seemed to think this was odd behavior for a girl, and nobody ever said a word to the teacher.

Even whiner girl decided to keep her mouth shut.

At recess, I was a goddess, especially among the boys. They all wanted to master my technique but never quite got it. They asked over and over again how I acquired my fly skills, and I tried to coach them as best I could.

"The best way to achieve ultimate fly catching is the two-handed method. By placing one hand on either side of the fly and waiting patiently for the right moment (achieved best while the fly is grooming himself), quickly bring your hands together as a trap. The hands need to come completely together like a puzzle or the fly will escape through the tiniest opening." Patience and practice – that's what the other students lacked.

Fall wore on, and the flies continued to come into the room. I continued to slither out of my desk and silently crawl across the room to catch one fly after the next. According to classmates who were keeping score, I was well into the fifties by now.

Upon entering class and slipping into my assigned desk one morning, I notice there wasn't a single fly in sight. My eyes glanced around the room and found nothing. Hmm. Maybe they all died off for the winter, I thought. Maybe I terminated all of them without realizing it.

Throughout the day I continued with my usual schoolwork but kept an eye out for a fly. There was nothing. How odd.

Lunch time.

As I walked toward the front of the room to line up for lunch Mrs. Friendshoe called me to her desk. She leaned in quietly so no one else could hear and said, "Elaine, I know what you've been up to and you've done it very quietly, but you are not paying attention to what's really important." She held up a flyswatter and grinned at me. "How about if you leave the flies to me now."

My face turned red and I smiled back at her. "Okay. Sorry Mrs. Friendshoe," and I turned to go to lunch.

In the afternoon, I was reading my social studies book when a fly landed on the page.

I just waved it off.

There was a new Flyminator in town.

Chapter 36

Northern Wildlife

During school breaks Martha and Royal often came down to the Cities and brought us up to Hibbing for a visit.

I was the only one able to go this time, so they picked me up late in the afternoon and we headed back up to Hibbing.

It was winter, so daylight disappeared early at that latitude.

We were driving down the desolate highway in pitch blackness when it began to snow lightly, making visibility a challenge.

Driving on the highways up north is the reverse of driving through South Dakota. Where South Dakota has miles and miles of endless prairie, northern Minnesota has miles and miles of thick tree forests that come within several feet of the highway. It's a bit unnerving in the dark because the wildlife is large and fast and comes out of nowhere.

We were the only ones on the road this particular night and hadn't seen another car for miles. It was getting late and I was tired, so I settled in the back seat to take a snooze when I heard Martha and Royal talking about a huge hole in the middle of the highway up ahead. Royal began to slow down just a bit.

"That seems odd that there would be just one huge hole when the rest of the road is fine," Royal said.

"Maybe you should just drive around it. It looks big enough to swallow the car," Martha suggested. "Do you think maybe it's a sink hole?"

"I think I can just center the car over the hole and not hit anything."

I laid back down in the back seat knowing that we would be fine, when suddenly, BAM! I was thrown into the back of the front seat as the car flew through the air and landed hard back on the highway. Royal brought the car to a screeching halt.

"What in the world was that?" Royal asked; visibly shaken.

We came to a complete stop in the middle of the road while we all took a minute to catch our breath.

"That wasn't a hole; I think we hit something lying in the road," Martha said.

Royal got out of the car to see what the damage was and noticed that the radiator was beginning to leak. He got back into the car and turned it around in the middle of the road in order to use the cars headlights and see what he hit.

Lying in the middle of the road was a young black bear!

Apparently, the poor bear had been hit by someone else who left it lying in the middle of the road. And what choice did the driver have? The bear probably weighed 200 pounds or more so there is no way of moving it without a tractor or a set of chains. Besides, it's never a good idea to get out of your car and check on a bear lying in the middle of the road to make sure he's dead. There's always the possibly that he could just be stunned. And angry!

Our car managed to limp the last twenty-five miles up to Hibbing without breaking down.

The radiator was destroyed as was most of the undercarriage. The mechanic said the car's underneath was coated with black hair and pieces of hide and that he had no idea how in the world we made it back without a tow.

Clearly someone was watching over us that night

Chapter 37

The Vacation

We took a once in a lifetime family vacation. It proved to be quite an adventure for all of us.

Since our move down to the Cities, none of us kids were very happy with our new environment. It would never be the same as living up in the woods. In order to ease our sadness (and for Dad to get some serious fishing in), our parents thought we could all use a vacation up north. Even further north than we had ever gone.

Canada!

So that we could travel with seven people, luggage, tents, camping supplies, fishing stuff, boats, etc., my parents actually bought a brand-new vehicle! It was a Volkswagen van that had two bucket seats in the front and two bench seats in the back like today's mini vans but with all the comfort of a school bus. We thought it was amazing!

We drove it to Mom's brother's farm in Zim where we spent the night and had some fun with our cousins. Before leaving, we had fun riding the horse and playing in the barn. Dad and Hillary welded a trailer hitch to the van so we could tow his boat and ours up to Canada.

Bright and early the next day we ate a hearty breakfast, re-packed the van, said our good-byes and headed north to Ontario on our one and only real family vacation. We kids were so excited we could hardly speak.

Zim is about as far north as you can get before crossing the border into another country, so there was absolutely NO traffic on the highway.

About 10 miles prior to crossing into Canada, Dad pulled over to lecture us.

"Alright you guys. We're about to go into another country and they will be stopping us at the border to make sure we are not taking anything across that could be illegal.

"While I'm talking to the border patrol, I don't want any of you to say ANYTHING! Got it? Let me handle this." We all nodded nervously, unsure of what Dad could be talking about. What would we be taking with us that could possibly be illegal? Wonder Bread? Twinkies?

Were we going to be arrested for crossing the border?

We started the car again and began driving down the road when out of the ditch came a mother skunk and her four tiny little babies. Dad stopped the car and we all went up to the windshield to get a closer look.

"Ohhh, they're adorable!"

"Gosh, are they ever cute!"

"Can we keep one?"

The mother skunk was clearly annoyed with her babies and with us for laughing and ogling her as she tried her best to get them all across the road. It must have been their first outing because the babies were having fun leaping over one another and rolling around on the highway.

We all laughed at the little cuties, but mama skunk didn't appreciate our laughter one bit! I don't know what she thought we were doing, but she was *not* happy!

Mama skunk finally got her rowdy little ones safely across the road and we were about to go on our way when she came back out of the ditch, ran over to us, lifted her tail and let the front tire have it at very close range.

Now readers, I don't know if you have ever had a close encounter with a skunk, but it's one of the worse smells your nose will ever sniff. Downright nauseating!

Cars were not air conditioned and we had to continue on our way with all the windows rolled up. It was getting pretty bad in the van.

When we reached the border crossing, Dad rolled down his window to talk to them.

"Good afternoon, sir," Dad said as he rolled down his window and choked on the putrid smell.

The border patrol was busy looking at his clipboard and didn't look up to greet my dad.

"Do you have any, (he choked as the breeze shifted in his direction)…Oh, my gosh, what happened to you?"

"We had a run-in with an angry mother skunk."

The officer tried his best to ask us all the required questions of his job but he could no longer stand the smell coming off our car.

"Agh, just go! Get out of here!" He waved us through with his clipboard.

So we crossed into Canada. All smiles.

"Well, that was easy," Dad said.

Chapter 38

Army Worms

My parents had made reservations at a campground on Lake of the Woods up in Kenora, Ontario and we were all excited for our vacation to begin.

Dad went to check us in and find out where our campsite was, but when he returned, the camp owner was with him and Dad was looking nervous.

"Sorry to tell you folks. I can't let you camp here."

"But we have reservations!" Mom said.

"I know, and I'm really sorry about that, but there is a terrible infestation of army worms this year so we're shutting down the campground until they die off. They're everywhere and they're driving people crazy." As he spoke, an army worm was crawling up the front of his shirt. Out of nowhere, one fell on his cap and was crawling laps around the man's head.

As funny as that looked, we all began to tear up at the loss of our long-awaited vacation.

Dad pulled the campground owner aside and said, "Look, this is the only vacation we have ever been able to afford, and we have been planning and looking forward to this for months. Isn't there something you can do to help us out?" Dad asked the camp owner.

"I'm sorry folks, I really am, but there's nothing I can do when it's an act of nature."

"How about other campgrounds?" Dad asked.

"You're welcome to try; I'm not charging you with a cancellation fee so you can try another place if you want to. It's my understanding though that these worms are all over the area for miles."

We all sat in the car looking stunned, trying to figure out what to do now.

Mom took the map out of the glove compartment to see if there were other campgrounds that we could try and find another place to camp.

"Are we going to have to go home, Mom?" I asked.

"I hope not. We've come too far to give up now. Just let us look for a new place," Mom said.

Just then the owner came trotting out of the office with a smile on his face.

"Wait! Folks, I can't let you stay here; but if you would like, the people who own the island over there are willing to let you rent the island for the next week and a half for the same price you were going to pay me. They just ask that you try not to bring any worms over there from here. The owners live on the island so please respect their privacy. They live on the other side so you probably won't see each other during your stay."

Our mouths all dropped.

"The whole island?" Nita said. "That's amazing!

We cheerfully agreed and began unpacking the van so we could load all of our belongings in the two fishing boats. Before casting off, we carefully checked everything from top to bottom to make sure there were no worm hitchhikers.

The island was a good size and we would be able to spend lots of time exploring when we weren't fishing.

We set up camp, then went back to where we left the car so we could go to town and get supplies.

Kenora looks a lot like any other northern Minnesota town with an abundance of pine trees, beautiful lakes and swampy areas. The people were very friendly and asked where we were from. They knew we weren't from around there because they said we all spoke with an accent. Nita and I thought that was funny since we thought *they* all had funny accents. Eh?

After we bought our supplies, we went out to the van and noticed a man with a bicycle, carefully eyeing our car.

"Where did you get this van?" he asked my mom.

At first we were afraid he thought we had stolen it, from the accusatory tone in his voice, so we were a little frightened of the strange man.

"We bought it in Minnesota," Mom said.

"I'd like to buy it from you," The man said.

"Sorry," Mom said. "It's not for sale."

"I'll pay you more that you paid for it if you'll sell it to me."

"I'm sorry," Mom said apologetically. "We're on vacation and we need this car to get back home. It's all we have, and we need to have something this size to get the seven of us and the boats back home."

The man wrote something on a piece of paper and handed it to Mom. It was his name and phone number. "If you change your mind, please give me a call. I'd sure love to have that van."

"Okay, well, thank you," Mom said and then we packed to go back to the island.

(In retrospect, the van turned out to be a real lemon. We should have sold it while we had the chance.)

That was that the last new car we ever had.

***

"Worm check!" Mom said as we finished loading the boats with supplies and heading back to camp.

We tossed several of them off our clothes, the boat, and our grocery bags before we left the shore and headed across the lake to our beautiful island.

On shore, we checked for worms again in case there were any hitch hikers. There were.

"We need to be really careful," Mom said. "These worms will eat every leaf off every tree on the island if they begin to spread. You have my permission to destroy them but don't let them on the island. "This was wasn't something mom would normally say since she didn't believe in hurting *any* creatures that weren't intended for food, so we knew these worms were a real problem. Even the fish wouldn't eat them.

***

We spent all day fishing the coves of the huge lake and went home each night with a delicious northern or two to cook over our open campfire. We caught several fish each day but released them. We couldn't eat them all but they each provided us with a wonderful story.

Even over an open flame, Mom was able to use her cooking magic and make a delicious meal for us.

One day she announced she was going to make a large pot of "bean-hole beans."

"What are those?" I asked.

"You'll see, but it's going to take several days to get them just right."

We dug a hole and placed a large covered pot inside the hole, covered it up and started a new fire over the bean pot.

"Now we just keep the fire going whenever we're on the island."

On the fourth day of fishing, Nita and I were getting a little tired of spending hours and hours on the lake. Fishing had lost its appeal and wasn't fun anymore.

"Can't we just stay here this evening while you guys go out?" Nita asked.

"I don't know," Mom said. "I don't really feel comfortable leaving you two all alone. What if you fall in the water? There's nobody around to help you."

"We promise not to go near the water, Mom." Nita said. "Besides, the water is so cold we wouldn't want to get in it anyway."

Mom and Dad talked it over and decided if we wore our lifejackets at *all times*, that we could stay on the island. "There are drop-offs and slippery rocks on the edge of the shore, and we don't want to risk having you slip into the water," Mom said.

Wow! What a surprise! We could stay alone as long as we wore our lifejackets? Sweet!

Mom, Dad and the boys all piled into the boats while Nita and I watched as they became no more than two tiny specks in the distance and the rumbling sound of their motors disappeared.

"Well, what shall we do, Nita?"

"Mom bought us some magazines and coloring books while we were in town. Let's start with that. She also said we could each have a small bag of sunflower seeds (that was a big deal). I'll go get them."

We chatted our little girl chat, colored and ate our sunflower seeds feeling very grown up.

As we looked over the lake toward the boat landing, the sun was beginning to set and we noticed something very strange. A large fin was swimming right up to shore.

"What in the world is that?" I asked Nita. We strained our eyes and squinted to see what was coming our direction through the water.

"I don't know; let's go look," she said as we scrambled down to the shoreline.

We got as close as we could without going into the water and watched as a northern continued to swim slowly to shore.

Danny had let a northern go the day before because it was too small and had swallowed the hook too badly. We wondered if this fish could possibly have swum across from the bay they were fishing in and into our landing. Probably not given the size of the lake, but it was a good guess.

"I know," I said. "Let's catch it and then we can show everyone that we didn't *need* to be in a boat to catch a fish!"

This sounded like a splendid idea so we looked around for the extra fishing net to catch the fish without scaring it away.

We carefully placed the net below the big fish and then swiftly lifted the net with the fish firmly in it! At last, all my turtle catching practice finally paid off!

"We caught it!" Nita cheered.

"We are the mighty shore fisher girls!" I said.

"Do we have a stringer so we can keep him and show Mom and Dad?" I asked.

She thought for a minute and then said, "I know, I saw one over by the tent." She ran to get it.

We put the stringer through the big fish's mouth and gill, tied the other end of the stringer to a tree branch. Next we put the fish back in the water and sat down with a sense of pride while we glowed, thinking about our big catch.

"They should be coming home soon," Nita said as she looked across the lake to see if she could see their boats.

"The sun is beginning to set so we need to watch for their lights and listen for the motors," I said.

Finally, we saw two sets of tiny little white, red and green lights coming across the big lake and could hear the hum of the fishing motors.

When the two boats containing our family landed, Nita and I could hardly contain our excitement over showing off our "land catch."

"How did you two catch that fish?" Mom laughed.

We explained what happened, and our parents thought we were very clever indeed.

"You didn't go in the water, did you?" Dad asked.

"No, we were both very careful and just let the fish come to us!" We explained.

"I'm afraid we can't eat it." Dad said. He may be sick, so we have to let it go."

"It's ok. We just had to show you what great 'land fishergirls' we are!" Nita said.

That night, Nita and I went to sleep with smiles on our faces.

Chapter 39

Visitors

We were now into day six of our camping/fishing trip and Nita and I had really had it with sitting quietly in a boat and fishing all day. With enough begging and pleading *and* reminders that we did exactly what Mom and Dad had said last time and didn't complain, we were able to stay on the island again while everyone else went fishing.

Mom made us sandwiches with chips, and we were each allowed to have a whole bottle of pop! We had never had pop before, so this was a rare treat indeed! To top it off, we each got another snack sized bag of sunflower seeds that we didn't have to share with one another. This was the life!

Mom said they would come home by 2:00 and then we would all do something together that didn't involve fishing.

We said our good-byes, Nita and I put on our "land lifejackets" and sat down with our bags of sunflower seeds.

"I think we should explore the island today," Nita said.

"Good idea! Do you think we might get lost though?"

"It's an island, the worst we can do is go around and around until Mom and Dad find us and bring us back to camp." Nita was so clever.

We finished our sunflower seeds, went to use the facilities, (which was really just branches lashed together like a goal post so we could hang on to something while we squatted over a hole in the ground) and then we began our journey to explore the island.

As we walked, we observed all the wildlife around us which basically consisted of birds, since everything else would have had to swim across the lake or come across the ice in the winter to get there.

Suddenly, Nita and I heard voices!

"Who could that possibly be?" I whispered as we ducked behind a tree. "I thought we were the only ones camping here."

"Remember, the guy at the campground said that the island belongs to someone on the other side from where we are."

"Do you think they're friendly?"

"How should I know? I don't even know who they are."

"Who's there?" A women's lilting voice asked.

We slowly came out from behind the tree.

A lovely white-haired woman stood in the middle of the path that lead around the island. She was wearing a calf-length chambray dress covered by a large white gardening apron with several large pockets. An oversized sun bonnet adorned her head. She had a potted plant in one hand and a trowel in the other. A smudge of dirt was across her cheek. She didn't exactly seem like a dangerous person – unless she planned on hitting us over the head with the flower pot.

"And who do we have here?" The kindly lady asked.

"I'm Nita."

"I'm Elaine.

"We're sisters."

"Oh, I see," the lady said. She pointed to our life jackets and asked, "Are you looking for a good place to go swimming?"

"Oh, no," Nita said. "We just promised our mom and dad that we would wear our life jackets while they're out fishing."

"Smart parents. And I'm glad to see you mind them. Did they ever tell you about not talking to strangers?" The lady asked.

Nita and I both looked very guilty and began to back up slowly in case we needed to make a run for it.

"It's ok," she said. "My husband and I are good friends with the campground owner. I spoke with your mom over the phone when they rented our island. My name is Mary," she said. "This handsome fellow here is my husband Harold." Harold was walking toward us down the path. He was medium height, thin, and had a very kindly look about him. They definitely looked like people who would prefer living on an island in Canada rather than a large city.

"What are you two doing out here all alone?"

"We've been here for a week now and all we have done every day is fish!" Nita said. "Frankly, we're getting a little tired of it and we're looking forward to going home."

"Well I can understand that," Mary concurred. "I would be a little tired of fishing as well."

"Would you like to join us for lunch?" Mary asked.

"Well, um," I said.

"Elaine had a scary close encounter with a stranger once, so she's a little worried about being with people she doesn't know."

"I'm sorry to hear about that, Elaine. How about if we eat lunch outside. Would that be better?" Mary offered.

"Well, sure, I guess that would be alright."

"Good," Harold said. "I'll help you carry everything out."

Soon lunch was served on the picnic table in the garden and we had a wonderful visit. Our hosts each had lovely British accents and it was fun to listen to them. We talked about school and how American schools and Canadian schools are the same and different; we talked about Cub Scouts (They called them Scout Cubs – isn't that funny?) We enjoyed hearing about our two different countries.

"Thanks, Mary and Harold. We had a great time and lunch was delicious!" I said. "Can we help you bring stuff inside?"

"Sure, that would be great," Mary said. We carried everything into the cabin. It was a lovely, warm cottage with a kitchen, fireplace and homey living area with knotty pine walls and lots of windows all around. It seemed so inviting after living in a tent for a week.

I looked at Mary hopefully and asked, "Do you have an indoor bathroom that we could use?"

"Why yes, we do," Mary smiled. "Are you getting a little tired of digging holes?"

"You have no idea," Nita said.

"You're welcome to use the bathroom before you leave if you would like."

"Oh, *thank* you!" I said.

We said our good-byes and thanked Mary and Harold again and went back to the campsite.

Chapter 40

The Big Storm

Out of nowhere, a fierce wind suddenly picked up and we ran around the camp site grabbing things and putting them in the tents to keep them from blowing away.

We looked out across the big lake and noticed the waves getting higher and clouds becoming more ominous. Lake of the Woods is a huge lake so when the wind comes up, it can really be terrifying. Nita and I were more than just a little scared by this time and we worried what would become of us if anything happened to our family.

"Do you think Mom and Dad and the boys will be ok?" I asked Nita.

"You know how cautious Dad is. I'm sure he has been watching the weather and they are on their way home."

Pretty soon we were able to see a tiny boat bobbing through the waves from across the lake.

"Here they come!" I shouted. "I can see a boat!"

"Can you see both boats?" Nita asked.

I strained to see across the lake.

"No. I only see one," I said softly.

We were suddenly very worried and not sure whose boat we were seeing.

We watched the boat bobbing up and down as it slowly came toward the island. At times the boat would disappear in the trough of the waves and we feared that the boat would not appear with the next crest. Nita and I were trying hard not to cry as the second boat failed to appear.

"Wait! Harold had a telescope back at the cabin. Maybe he could look out at the lake and find the other boat," I said.

We ran to the cabin and breathlessly explained what was happening.

Harold said he would be glad to watch for the other boat while we went back to the landing to see who was coming in our direction.

Finally, the boat landed safely on shore. It was Mom and Dad!

Nita and I gave out a cry of relief.

We flew into their arms when the boat was securely docked.

"Where are the boys?" I asked.

"We don't know," Mom said nervously. "They were right behind us and then they just disappeared!"

"You have to go back and look for them!" I said frantically.

"We can't," Dad said. "The weather is too rough. We need to pray that they can land on an island until this storm passes."

"Harold is watching for them with his telescope. We should go see if he has seen anything."

"Who is Harold?" Dad asked.

"I'll explain later – follow us!" I said.

Nita and I took off down the path toward Mary and Harold's with Dad and Mom following close behind. The wind was blowing so hard by now that we had to lean into it to avoid being blown over.

"Hi! You must be the parents of these two fine young ladies," Harold shouted.

"Yes, they said you have a telescope and that you may have been watching for the boys."

"Yes, I've been watching carefully on the water where you came across and I think I might see something coming in our direction. It disappeared for so long in the waves that I wasn't sure exactly what I was looking at but I'm pretty sure it's a boat."

"Oh, I sure hope you're right," Dad said.

"Wait a minute!" Harold said. "It's them! There are definitely three people on board. The motor is up so they must have had some trouble.

Harold returned to his telescope and then looked at Dad and asked, "Did they have a yellow poncho?"

Mom and Dad looked quizzically at one another.

"Yes, they did! We heard that the weather could get rough, so we made sure that they all had their ponchos. Gary's was yellow."

"Well, it looks like they have lashed the oars together and tied the poncho to it and they're using it as a sail." Harold took another careful look at the boys, smiled, and said, "I think they're fine – they're laughing and having a great time!"

With that, Mom and Dad burst into laughter.

"Leave it to those guys to figure out how to get back," Mom said.

They continued to watch as the boys' boat came closer.

The boys were laughing and whooping it up as they neared the shore. They were coming full steam ahead under poncho power.

They landed on the island with a thump tossing Danny and Gary out of the boat. The boys jumped up laughing and clearly excited over their big adventure.

"Did you see us?" Gary asked. "That was amazing!"

"What in the world happened to you guys?" Dad asked.

"A huge wave came over the boat and our motor died shortly after we left from the fishing area," Danny said. "We didn't know what to do. You couldn't hear us yelling for you over the wind so we had no way of letting you know we were in trouble. Then David suggested we sail home. It was so exciting! David held the center oar in place and stuck his head through the hood of the poncho so he could direct us while Gary and I maneuvered the horizontal oar." The boys were clearly excited!

David just stood and smiled. I think he was both proud ... and in shock. After all, it was he who saved the day and possibly the lives of the three of them.

The boys were safe.

We introduced everyone to our "island mates" and all was right with the world.

***

The next day we went out as a family and did some exploring of the Kenora area just as Mom and Dad had promised. No fishing!

On our return, we fried up some more fish, dug out the bean hole beans and invited Mary and Harold to join us.

***

The next day we packed up our belongings, said our good-byes and headed back to Minnesota.

It was an unforgettable time together.

It never happened again, but it was the best vacation anyone could ever hope to have.

Chapter 41

Years later

After moving to the suburbs of St. Paul, I felt lost and misplaced. Even though the area was still mainly farmland, it wasn't *my* farmland. I wasn't free to roam on other people's property, to roam *their* woods, to play with *their* animals, to help with *their* chores. On occasion, my siblings and I would politely ask a farmer if we could cross his property or swim in his pond. But it wasn't the woods or lakes from up north. The trees were largely oak, and we missed the pine trees of the North Country that reached high up to the sky. There is no scent to an oak tree.

Lakes in the Cities lacked the size and clarity of water that we were used to.

None of us ever moved back up north although Dan went to school at Bemidji State and now lives in the warmth of Hawaii. He is still filled with nostalgia whenever he has an opportunity to go to Chisholm, Hibbing and Cohasset.

After a time in New York City and Wisconsin, David and his family eventually moved back to the Cities and lived a few miles from our home in Eagan.

His wife's family owned a cabin in the Upper Peninsula of Michigan, so he frequently enjoyed time in the north woods and enjoyed watching the bears, wolves and other wildlife. Sadly, he recently passed away from ALS and dementia.

After burying most of his ashes in a beautiful cemetery overlooking the Mississippi River Valley near Eagan, the family ventured up to Chisholm to put some of David's ashes on our mother's grave before sprinkling the rest at the lake cabin.

As the rest of the family began to leave the cemetery and return to their homes in the Cities, our son Ben, my husband Randy and I drove around Chisholm so I could proudly show him where I grew up and where my grandparents lived.

The home which my uncle so meticulously painted every other year for Grandma and Grandpa was gone. It had fallen victim of a meth lab gone wrong and it blew up right on its foundation. The houses my family lived in in Chisholm were still occupied and looked exactly as we had left them.

We drove down the road to Hibbing to take a look at Martha and Royal's place. It looked a bit run-down and Martha's beautiful flowers, vegetable garden and yellow rose bushes were long gone.

Since we were already up north, we decided we couldn't leave without going over to Cohasset so my family could see where all the stories of my youth originated.

I had managed to make the trip to Cohasset a few times over the years when I visited Martha and Royal so I could see the old place again.

On one trip, the trailer park was completely closed and cordoned off with wire cable. The house owned by the trailer court owner had apparently burned to the ground so the place was overgrown with weeds and wildflowers.

The second time it didn't look much better but this time it was a trailer park again with a half dozen trailers occupying various lots. It was good to see life in the old place.

Ben and Randy were good sports as I walked them around the area where our trailer stood. There was no longer a path through the fields leading to the swimming hole. In fact, the entire river had disappeared as well! We could barely see where the water once flowed because of the weed and tree overgrowth.

Looking into the trough as best I could, I realized just how deep the river had been in some places. Apparently, the Bass River had been dammed up coming from the lake because there wasn't so much as a drop of water anywhere near the park.

The trailers in the park had all seen better days and appeared to be from the same era that ours was many years ago. The people all appeared to be happy but a bit down on their luck – much like so many of our old neighbors.

I felt a little embarrassed describing the place we loved so much to Ben and Randy and then showing them what it looks like now. They humored me though as they looked at the run-down area and smiled. To me it was still wonderful! It felt like home again.

It was hard to describe to them where we built our tree house and exactly where everything was when we were kids, but in my mind I knew exactly where everything was so many years ago.

Everything changes over time.

My family and I decided it was time to head back to the Cities.

As we made our way back down the country highway that would eventually connect to a main artery taking us down to the Cities after the sprinkling ceremony, I noticed a very large animal desperately trying to make its way through a thick forest of aspen trees.

At first, I thought it was a moose but then a huge black bear emerged from the woods and stood watching us as we drove by. I can't help but believe that it was David's way of saying "good-bye" and "thanks" for returning him to the place he loved so much.

...

I have moved back to South Dakota for the third time, but I miss the lakes and trees of Minnesota every day. I would go back in a heartbeat.

Life *is* what you make of it. I am glad that I had the opportunity to grow up poor but not deprived in the woods where I learned so much about nature; that I acquired survival skills and learned how to use common sense in tough situations.

I love that all big trees are for climbing and that I seldom missed an opportunity to try one out. Looking back, I can't say I would have allowed my own children all the latitude that we were given.

But then times were different.

Acknowledgements

I would like to give a special thanks to all the friends, family and students who volunteered to read this book and for all their insight in writing it. Mary, you rock! I wish I had had you as an English teacher way back when. Also to Rolan Wengert and his magic, technical fingers.

A very special thanks to my husband and kids who listened to these stories over and over and provided me with a huge amount of support.

I appreciate the assistance I received from the owners of Daisy Bay Resort, The Minnesota Museum of Mining and the Hibbing Chamber of Commerce.

I also owe a huge thank you to my 4th, 5th and 6th grade students at Legacy Elementary in Tea, SD, Tea Area Middle School, and Journey Elementary School in Harrisburg, SD for encouraging me to put my stories into print.

Thanks for helping me to make this happen, guys!

Open spaces are so very important to our well-being. Take time to hike, camp and learn more about the world around us.

Above all, be good to your surroundings!

CPSIA information can be obtained
at www.ICGtesting.com
Printed in the USA
BVHW071438171220
595872BV00013B/868